The Ancient World: Source Books

General Editor: Peter Walcot
Professor of Classics, University of Cardiff

Democracy: Ideas and Realities

Edited with an Introduction by
COSMO RODEWALD
Senior Lecturer in History, University of Manchester

Dent, London
Hakkert, Toronto

© Introduction, translations and commentary,
J. M. Dent & Sons Ltd, 1974

All rights reserved
Made in Great Britain
at the
Aldine Press · Letchworth · Herts
for
J. M. DENT & SONS LTD
Aldine House · Albemarle Street · London
First published in 1975

Published in Canada, the United States of
America and its dependencies by A. M. HAKKERT LTD,
554 Spadina Crescent, Toronto M5s 2J9,
Canada

This book if bound as a paperback is
subject to the condition that it may not
be issued on loan or otherwise except in
its original binding

This book is set in
9 on 10 and 10 on 11 point Fournier 185

Dent edition
Hardback ISBN 0 460 10302 4
Paperback ISBN 0 460 11302 X

Hakkert edition
Hardback ISBN 0 88866 569 5
Paperback ISBN 0 88866 570 9

Foreword

Although few today study Greek and Latin at school or college, there has never been a more widespread interest in classical civilization and culture. How academically respectable is such an interest unless it is reinforced by an ability to read the Greek and Latin languages? Certainly it is crucially important that a student should have a direct contact with the primary evidence, that is, the evidence offered by what our ancient authorities say themselves. Yet this need may be met by the provision of sound translations, for these can go a long way towards supplying an acceptable alternative to an actual knowledge of Greek and Latin. It is no longer possible to argue, as it was possible in antiquity, that a man can attain mastery of all branches of learning; the sheer complexity of the modern world forces us to be selective in education as in so much else. It is not reasonable to expect the student to be conversant with a variety of languages, but it would be absurd if we restricted our studies to the exclusive consideration of those speaking and writing our native tongue. In fact, if an effort to guide a student's interest is to be really constructive, we are obliged to do more than just supply adequate translations; we must also be willing to collect together as representative a selection of the relevant evidence in translation as is possible. What then is left to the student? A great deal. Questions are posed and evidence is presented, but the student finds the answers himself. The student must think for himself, and his thoughts will not be casual or ill-founded if he and his colleagues can and do make frequent reference to the primary evidence which it is the purpose of this series of source-books to collect and to translate.

PETER WALCOT

Contents

Foreword   v
Preface   xi
Note on Proper Names and Dates   xii
Select Bibliography   xiii
Introduction   xv

I. REALITIES OF GREEK DEMOCRACY: ATHENS IN THE FIFTH AND FOURTH CENTURIES

Xenophon, *History of Greece* 1.7	2
Aristotle, *Constitution of Athens* 42–69 (extracts)	6
Demosthenes, *On the Crown* 169–170	11
Aischines, *Against Timarchos* 27–32	12
Plato, *Gorgias* 455–459	13
Xenophon, *Memoirs* 3.7	14
Aristophanes, *Women in Assembly* 376–461	15
Andokides, *On the Mysteries* 82–87	20
Demosthenes, *Against Timokrates* 19–24, 32–34, 37, 138, 152–154	21
[Demosthenes], *Against Neaira* 2–8, 13, 88–92, 114–115	24
Aischines, *Against Ktesiphon* 9–21	27
Aristophanes, *Wasps* 548–691	29
Aristophanes, *Wealth* 899–925	32
Lysias 21.1–5, 10–19	34
Aristotle, *Politics* 6.2	36

II. ORIGINS OF GREEK DEMOCRACY: FROM THERSITES TO TYRTAIOS

Homer, *Odyssey* 2.1–81, 224–239 (extracts); 9. 106–115	40
Iliad 2.179–181, 207–282	41
Hesiod, *Works and Days* 202–285	44

Aristotle, *Politics* 4.13	46
Tyrtaios, Fragment 9	48
Aristotle, *Politics* 5.7	49
Tyrtaios, Fragment 3	50
Thucydides 1.88	50
Aristotle, *Politics* 2.9	51
Xenophon, *History of Greece* 3.3	53

III. DEMOCRACY AND SOCIETY: ATHENS AND SYRACUSE

Aristotle, *Constitution of Athens* 2–3, 5, 11–12	57
Solon, Fragments 4–5, 23, 24–25	57
Aristotle, *Politics* 2.12	61
Constitution of Athens 20–22	62
Thucydides 1.93, 107	64
Plato, *Laws* 4.707	65
[Xenophon], *Constitution of Athens* 1–3 (extracts)	66
Thucydides 6.89	70
Aristotle, *Constitution of Athens* 27, 41	71
Xenophon, *Ways and Means* (extracts)	73

IV. ATTITUDES TO DEMOCRACY IN GREECE

Pindar, *Pythian Odes* 2.81–89	77
Aischylos, *The Suppliant Women* 365–949 (extracts)	79
Herodotos 5.78; 5.97; 3.80–83	80
Euripides, *The Suppliant Women* 399–441	82
Plato, *Protagoras* 322–323	84
Demokritos, Fragments 251, 255	85
Thucydides 2.34–41 (extracts); 6.37–39	85
Aristophanes, *Knights* 147–193, 725–755, 1111–1150	89
Xenophon, *Memoirs* 1.2	92
Lysias 25.1–3, 7–14	95
Isokrates, *Areopagiticus* 16, 20–21, 26, 70	98
On the Peace 52, 64	100
Thucydides 2.8; 3.47; 8.48	100
Aristotle, *Politics* 5.1; 6.4; 5.9; 3.11; 6.3	104

V. DEMOCRACY AND EMPIRE: ALEXANDER AND AFTER

Decree of the Samians	108
Polybios 2.37–42 (extracts); 28.7; 22.11; 10.22	110

Contents

    Pausanias 7.14   115
    Polybios 38.9–10; 39.11   115
    Pausanias 7.16–17   117

VI. THE PERFECT DEMOCRACY OF THE ROMAN EMPIRE

    Cicero, *In Defence of Flaccus* 16–19   118
    Philostratos, *Life of Apollonios of Tyana* 5.35–36   120
    Aristides, *To Rome* 90, 59–60, 63   121
    Dio Cassius 52.30   122
    Decree of the Chalkidians   123
    Edict of the Emperor Constantine   124
    Libanios, *Speeches* 11.133, 150–152; 29.2, 4; 11–12;   124
        26.5, 8

Notes   128
Index   135

Preface

In putting this book together I have lived with the relevant texts and documents rather than with the work of modern writers, but my debt, conscious or unconscious, to books and articles that I have read at one time or another is naturally great. I hope that those who sense that I have used, perhaps misused, their work will accept this general acknowledgment. I am indebted also to previous translators of most of the texts. My purpose in making new versions has not been to outdo them in accuracy, let alone literary quality, but to bring out as clearly as possible what is relevant to the subject.

Peter Walcot, who invited me to undertake the work, has read the entire typescript and made some useful suggestions; he must not be blamed for the errors that remain or for my views. But my largest debt is to my colleagues and, above all, my pupils in the Department of History at Manchester University, from whom I have gradually learnt what questions should be asked about ancient society and how one may set about answering them.

COSMO RODEWALD

Note on Proper Names and Dates

The Greek spelling has been followed in all cases except for a small number of familiar names which have an established English equivalent: Homer, Hesiod, Pindar, Thucydides, Socrates, Plato, Aristotle, Darius, Philip, Vespasian, Athens, Rhodes, Antioch and Cyclops. All dates referring to the ancient world are B.C., unless A.D. is prefixed.

Select Bibliography

Short articles, mostly excellent and mostly with a bibliography, on almost every person and institution named in this book can be found in the *Oxford Classical Dictionary* (Oxford, 2nd edn, 1970). Unfortunately, the majority of books and articles that go deeper into matters that have been touched on here assume a knowledge of Greek or Latin. The following, however, do not:

Finley, M. I. *Democracy Ancient and Modern* (London and New York, 1973).

Ehrenberg, V. *The Greek State* (London and New York, 2nd edn, 1969).

Sinclair, T. A. *A History of Greek Political Thought* (London, 2nd edn, 1967).

Larsen, J. A. O. 'Cleisthenes and the Development of the Theory of Democracy at Athens' in *Essays in Political Theory Presented to G. H. Sabine* (Ithaca, New York, 1948).

Jones, A. H. M. *Athenian Democracy* (Oxford, 1957).

Connor, W. R. *The New Politicians of Fifth Century Athens* (Princeton, 1971).

Finley, M. I. 'Athenian Demagogues' in *Past and Present* 1962.

Jones, A. H. M. *The Greek City from Alexander to Justinian* (Oxford, 1940).

Larsen, J. A. O. *Representative Government in Greek and Roman History* (Berkeley, 1955).

Staveley, E. S. *Greek and Roman Voting and Elections* (London and New York, 1972).

de Ste Croix, G. E. M. *The Class Struggle in the Ancient World* (London, 1975).

Gelzer, M. *The Roman Nobility* (Oxford, 1969).
Macmullen, Ramsay. *Enemies of the Roman Order* (Harvard, 1967).
Starr, Chester G., Jr. 'The Perfect Democracy of the Roman Empire' in *American Historical Review* 58 (1952).

Introduction

The Greeks had a word for it: *demokratia*, control by the People. For them, however, the thing came before the word, before the concept. It came as the result of what Popper has called 'piecemeal social engineering'[1]: those who led the way led by devising arrangements to remedy what seemed to them to have gone wrong with the established order, not by attempting to put a new order in its place.

To say this is not to deny what it is, indeed, equally important to recognize: that behind the successive modifications of the established order that led to participatory democracy there was adventurous, probing thought about how society works, how men ought to behave in society, how a community ought to be organized, thought which influenced, to some extent at least, those who used the new arrangements. However, the further that thinking about politics and society progressed towards what can be called political philosophy, the less influence it had, generally speaking, on what was done.

This brings us to the question: why in Greece did 'piecemeal social engineering' not remain confined to tinkering with the established order, the traditional rule of noble lords? Why did it lead to democracy, there being absolutely no precedents for such a transformation?

The basic factor surely was that each Greek community, each *polis*, that underwent this transformation remained relatively small and compact throughout. Every change took place within a group of a few thousand persons living at close quarters in the small town and the narrow stretch of surrounding countryside that together constituted a Greek *polis*,[2] a state on the scale of Andorra or Liechtenstein or San Marino or, at the largest, Costa Rica, but far more self-sufficient than any of these.

[1] Karl Popper, *The Open Society and its Enemies* (1945), I. 1 and passim.
[2] The plural form of this word is *poleis*.

Already in earlier stages of civilization small states had flourished for a time, particularly in Mesopotamia; but most of the innovations of the third and second millennia were made, in Asia or in Egypt, in larger-scale societies ruled by more or less despotic monarchs, who raised themselves, and the privileged minority assisting them, increasingly far above the level of the peasants and craftsmen on whose surplus production they depended. During the third millennium, inhabitants of the lands around the Aegean began to have regular contact with states of this kind that bordered on the Mediterranean, through sea trade, and later also through the journeyings of craftsmen, pirates, mercenaries and envoys; and thereafter the men who had raised themselves to the position of rulers in the communities of the Aegean naturally took these more elaborate Eastern states and societies as models in shaping their own economies and systems of rule: first in Crete, from 3000, in the civilization which we call Minoan, and then in the more widely spread Mycenean civilization which largely absorbed it and displaced it, and was at its most brilliant between 1400 and 1200.

However, the kings who between them ruled much of European Greece and some of the Greek islands during these centuries raised the superstructure of Mycenean civilization on more skimped and precarious foundations than those on which the greater kingdoms of the Near East rested, and during the twelfth century, in troubles caused partly by movements of less civilized peoples into the lands and seas of Greece and the Near East, the superstructure collapsed and completely disintegrated. Most of the Greek palaces were violently destroyed, the royal families went under, the offices, factories and stores attached to the palaces were abandoned, and those who had worked in them went back, if they survived, to trying to scrape a living from the soil. Some people fled from the districts hardest hit, and some of these eventually made themselves new homes, particularly on the coast of western Asia Minor and the adjacent islands. Meanwhile, kindred but more primitive peoples, who had probably been living to the north of Greece during the previous centuries, moved into some of the devastated areas; but the population of the areas that had been most prosperous remained for a long time much smaller than it had been.

It was in little self-sufficient communities that Greeks stuck together, or were held together by petty princes, through these hard

Introduction

times; for, unlike Mesopotamia and Egypt and most of the regions between them, the lands in which they were living are split into small units by mountains or rough hills and by the sea, and for a time no one dynasty had the strength to keep or bring any considerable number of such units under its rule. And in the relatively settled centuries that followed the period of destruction and disturbance, each such community had time to acquire self-consciousness and solidarity. Both lords and commoners were chiefly preoccupied with their own households, great or small; but when they had occasion to look beyond their own households they were aware of belonging to a group of households, working a certain area of land, with which they must not let outsiders interfere.

Here, then, are the roots of Greek democracy. Each of these little communities had at its head, to begin with, a prince, a *basileus*, and later a group of lords who regarded themselves as his peers, and who had decided, as life became more settled, that they no longer needed an overlord. These princes and lords believed that the blood that flowed in their veins set them apart from the rest of the community; but there was no great divide, in wealth or way of life or even, probably, in attitudes, between them and their subjects. All who belonged to the community felt that they counted for something, even if the commoners showed some deference to their lords. The great divide was between them and those who lived within the community's boundaries but were not regarded as belonging.

Slaves and serfs did not belong; nor did those who came from outside to settle for one reason or another: indeed, generations later the descendants of such immigrants might still not be accepted and might therefore still be forbidden to marry into the community or to own land. And there might be others who were excluded: those, for instance, who were already living in an area in which a group of Greeks succeeded in settling and creating a new *polis* for themselves. In most, if not all, Greek communities women also did not fully belong, inasmuch as they had no political rights and their civic rights were limited; but the wedded wives and the legitimate daughters of those who did belong had a status far superior to that of other women.

Things that happened during the eighth and seventh centuries gave some commoners a stronger sense of counting for something. A new mode of warfare which was gradually devised made moderately prosperous peasants who had no special skill scarcely less important than noblemen for the community's defence. There was an upsurge of travel, especially by sea, within and beyond the Aegean; and this meant that many other commoners, who could not get an adequate living from the land, came to hear of regions overseas in which they could create, with the help, perhaps, of some discontented nobleman, new communities with wider opportunities, while yet others turned to making a living as traders or as pirates, or as soldiers of fortune, serving great kings of the East. An alphabetic script invented by the Phoenicians, with whom Greeks were now in frequent contact, was borrowed and adapted, probably by traders, to suit the Greek language, so that the art of writing, which in Mycenean Greece had probably been the preserve of learned clerks in royal service, and had afterwards been forgotten, could now be mastered by ordinary men. Freer travel meant also a freer movement of ideas, loosening men's outlooks—though not to the point of engendering a will to revolutionary change in the social order.

In these circumstances some nobles were likewise impelled to break through traditional limits, not in order to go their own way, but in order to outdo their fellows, to get more than their fair share of the power, wealth and prominence desired by all. To this end, some succeeded in making themselves masters of their little communities; and since there was no sanction in *nomos*, in custom, for their seizure and exercise of despotic power, as there had been for the exercise by the *basileus* of a much more limited power, a new word, *tyrannos*, was coined to describe them.

Self-assertiveness, then, and, among the nobility, the urge to do better than one's fellows in some sense, are among the most important characteristics of the Greeks. But there is evidence also of a strong will to cooperate. It was the precarious balance between these two impulses, present in differing proportions, naturally, in each each individual, that gave the Greek *polis* and Greek democracy, when it arrived, their particular flavour. This may be thought a banal observation: these two impulses, it may be said, can be seen at work in every society. However, life at close quarters in a small community made men fully aware of the consequences of acting on one or other of these impulses; this perhaps strengthened both of them and increased the tension between them.

In suggesting how one may explain the movement of Greek com-

Introduction

munities towards democracy, we have raised a further question: why did not something similar happen at Rome? For in the sixth and fifth centuries Rome was a community that resembled many Greek communities in size and, superficially at least, in structure. To answer this question we do not need to play 'national character', although by the time at which we can get to know the Romans, at least of the ruling class, tolerably well—that is to say in the second and first centuries— there was, as the Romans themselves believed, a Roman national character quite distinct from the Greek character. For there is another difference, apparent much earlier. Whereas each Greek community, each *polis*, remained relatively small and compact, and whereas, if one *polis* gained ascendancy over another, the tendency was to subordinate rather than incorporate, the Romans incorporated other communities. They did so spasmodically but, in the long run, on a grand scale. They also admitted to citizenship most of the numerous slaves whom they liberated. The larger the Roman community thus grew, the less likely movement towards democracy of the Greek sort became.

It can, of course, be argued that in pointing to this difference in political behaviour one is pointing to a difference in attitudes. The Roman nobles seem to have been more willing to admit into their ranks elements from the ruling classes of other communities, together with occasional recruits, carefully selected by themselves, from within their own community, than to give more power to the People; and, to judge from events (since we have little direct evidence for what ordinary Romans thought), the People generally acquiesced, so long as the nobles governed successfully, and upheld the rule of law—thus ensuring for every member of the community what the Romans meant by *libertas*—and so long as individual nobles looked after those commoners who gave them their allegiance.

So perhaps we have discovered, after all, evidence for the existence, at an early date, of a difference in character between Greeks and Romans, Roman society being more paternalistic and authoritarian. Anyhow, since piecemeal social engineering did not bring about, at Rome, any change in political arrangements that was felt to be fundamental, it was not accompanied by increasingly sophisticated thinking about political principles; rather by an accumulation of precedents and patterns—how such and such a person behaved, how such and such a situation was handled; and Roman 'ideas', so far as they are not simply borrowed from Greeks, are largely about the following of such precedents and patterns, and about the observance of ties, between stronger and weaker, older and younger, benefactor and beneficiary.

The student of modern politics who looked at the index before reading this Introduction can now, I hope, see why one key word, participation, is missing from it: participation is a theme that runs right through the book. In the societies with which it is concerned, the usual alternative was patronage, rather than representation: that is why representation has so few entries against it. Parties are missing altogether, for they did not exist. So are classes, for, although classes did perhaps exist, use of the word in studies of these societies tends to be misleading rather than helpful.[1] But rich and poor will be with us throughout; so will nobles (or notables) and commoners; and so will slaves.

Slaves and serfs were mentioned above among those who did not belong to the communities within which they lived: these being the terms commonly used to comprehend all those at the darker end of what M. I. Finley has called 'a whole spectrum of statuses' within Greek and Roman society. This is not the place to analyse this spectrum. What is important for our purpose is to bear in mind that in every community there were men and women who were not free, who, although in some cases they had a measure of protection from cruel treatment, were obliged to do what their masters told them to do. Could democracy have been attained and maintained without them? Does their existence make a mockery of Greek claims to have achieved democracy?

Only a few things can be said here by way of answer to these questions. First: there was one Greek community, Sparta (of which we shall be hearing more in chapter II), in which those who belonged were wholly freed from productive work because there were unfree persons, helots, to do the work for them; and for this very reason Sparta could take, and had to take, as we shall see, some steps towards democracy before any other community had done so. But Sparta was exceptional. At Athens, the other community about which we know most, one of the first steps taken, not long afterwards, towards democracy was the liberation of a large number of unfree persons whom debt

---

[1] M. I. Finley explains why, in chapter II of *The Ancient Economy* (1973).

Introduction

had placed in bondage; thereafter they belonged fully to the community. Other slaves at Athens remained slaves, but at that time, the beginning of the sixth century, they were few; they became relatively numerous (though perhaps never to the point of outnumbering Athenians) only after the decisive steps towards democracy had been taken. Moreover a large proportion of them, at Athens and in other Greek states, were household servants, often unproductively employed, almost, in some cases, status symbols; and there was no branch of productive work—except silvermining—which they dominated, or in which they performed unpleasant tasks shunned by Athenians. But it is fair to say that Athenian democracy could not have had within it such intensity of political activity as it had between the later years of the fifth century and the later years of the fourth—the period illustrated by chapter I—if the Athenians had not had numerous slaves.[1] On the other hand, democracy of essentially the same kind, albeit less enterprising and with less participation, could have continued if all the slaves had vanished (though not if they had all been freed and made citizens); it did exist in many states in which slaves seem to have been relatively far fewer.

But is it right to describe as a democracy a community such as Athens, in which there are not merely guest-workers whose presence is voluntary but outsiders who are compelled to stay and work? That is surely a question of definition: not important if the facts are frankly recognized. One thing which needs to be borne in mind in assessing the influence of slavery on men's outlooks is that it was taken completely for granted, on both sides. What may seem to us the rather feeble efforts of Aristotle, in Book I of his *Politics*, to justify it philosophically must not be taken to indicate that there was a movement for the abolition of slavery (let alone that any movements anywhere towards democracy had any connection with such an idea). Later some philosophers came round to arguing (what plain men had long since accepted) that slaves are 'just like us'; but it was not suggested that they should cease to be slaves, or that, if one liberated a slave of whom one was particularly fond, one should not buy another to replace him.

To sum up: it is probably fair to say that without slavery the Greeks would not have gone as far as they did go towards democracy, to-

---

[1] See G. E. M. de Sainte-Croix, *Classical Review* 1957, 57–9.

wards freedom and equality, in their lives or in their thoughts. In an age of limited technical development there is a better chance of arriving at a democratic political system and a democratic social atmosphere if there are persons who stand outside the community altogether, and especially if some of the outsiders are not free, so that their productive capacity can be (although it not always is) exploited further than that of free men.

I. Realities of Greek Democracy: Athens in the Fifth and Fourth Centuries

THE PEOPLE IN ACTION

The best way of finding out what democracy meant in the ancient world is to observe it in action, at the time and the place at which it attained its fullest development—Athens at the end of the fifth century and during the fourth century B.C. It has been said that by the end of the fifth century the Athenians had stretched the notion of a direct democracy (as distinct from a representative system) about as far as was possible outside Utopia. Probably more of them were more actively involved in politics at that time than at any other; for in earlier generations fewer felt sufficiently self-confident, and so more was left to the old ruling class of noble landowners; while a generation or so later feelings were running less high and for most of the time fewer felt sufficiently interested, so that more was left to a new governing class, the professional politicians.

The events that are described below, by a man who had probably witnessed them, occurred in 406 after a crucial naval battle. This battle was the culmination of a great effort which the Athenians made, after a series of grave setbacks, to regain control of the Aegean from their enemies. The Athenian fleet was victorious, but many sailors who had been serving on Athenian ships that were wrecked had been left to drown. (The fundamental reason for the concern of the Athenians with naval power, and for the consequent need to let the poorer citizens, from among whom sailors for the fleet were largely drawn, participate as much as they might wish in the running of the community, was that Athens had become dependent on imported grain, which came mainly from the north of the Aegean, the Black Sea and Egypt. Thus a disastrous naval defeat one year later put the Athenians for a time entirely at the mercy of their main enemies, the Spartans, who were also in general enemies of democracy.)

Xenophon's story of what happened at Athens in August 406 illustrates most of the main features of Greek democracy in its fullest development: decisions by mass meeting, the Assembly, or *Ekklesia*, after discussion in which all may participate and present motions; preparation of business by a smaller, representative body chosen by lot, the Council, or *Boule*; choice of most officials by lot, but election by show of hands of a board of military commanders, the Generals, or *Strategoi*, and one or more financial supervisors; stringent popular control over all officials; accountability also of private citizens who gave advice in the Assembly; popular administration of justice. It also illustrates the rôle of leadership, in which nobles like Euryptolemos are now rivalled by commoners; the importance of oratorical skill for those aspiring to leadership; and a recognition, not yet, however, general, that the satisfactory working of such a system requires the imposition of checks of some kind on impulsive popular decisions.

Xenophon, *History of Greece* 1.7

Back home, the People removed from office all the Generals except Konon. Two of the Generals who had taken part in the battle, Protomachos and Aristogenes, did not return to Athens. When the other six—Perikles,[1] Diomedon, Lysias, Aristokrates, Thrasyllos and Erasinides—arrived, Archedemos, who was at that time a leading popular politician and Controller of the War-Relief Fund,[2] proposed the imposition of a fine on Erasinides and brought him before a Court of Justice, on a charge of having in his possession money from the Hellespont which belonged to the People;[3] he also preferred a charge relating to Erasinides' conduct as General. The Court decided that Erasinides should be remanded in custody. After this the Generals made statements at a meeting of the Council about the battle and the violence of the storm. Timokrates then proposed that these Generals too should be taken into custody and brought before the Assembly, and the Council had them taken into custody.

Afterwards there was a meeting of the Assembly, at which a number of people, and in particular Theramenes, attacked the Generals, saying that they should be called on to explain why they had not rescued the men who had been shipwrecked. As evidence that the Generals held no-one else responsible, Theramenes showed a letter which they had sent to the Council and the People, in which they put the whole blame on the storm. Each of the Generals then spoke in his own defence—briefly, for they were not offered the opportunity to deliver a speech as the law required.[4] They explained what had happened: they themselves were to sail in pursuit of the enemy, and they had given the job of rescuing the shipwrecked to some of the ship-captains, who were capable men and had served as Generals in the past—Theramenes, Thrasybulos and others of like ability. If anyone must be blamed, there was no-one whom they could blame for the failure of the rescue operations other than those to whom the job had been given. 'And we shall not', they added, 'make the false assertion that they are to blame, just because they are now making charges against us. We maintain that it was the violence of the storm that made the rescue impossible.' For this they offered as witnesses the helmsmen and many others who had sailed with them. With such arguments they were on the point of convincing the Assembly; many citizens were standing up and offering to go bail for them. However, it was decided that the matter should be adjourned to another meeting of the Assembly, for by then it was late and it would have been impossible to count votes, and that the Council should draft a motion as to what sort of trial the men should have.

After this came the Apaturia festival, at which fathers and their families meet together. Thus Theramenes and his supporters were able to arrange for men dressed in black and with their hair close-shaven, of whom there were large numbers at the festival, to attend the Assembly, as if they were kinsmen of those who had perished; and they induced Kallixenos to attack the Generals in the Council. Then came the meeting of the Assembly, at which the Council presented its motion, which was moved by Kallixenos. It was in the following terms: 'Resolved, that, since speeches in accusation of the Generals and speeches of the Generals in their own defence have been heard at the previous Assembly, all the Athenians do now proceed to hold a ballot by constituencies; that for each constituency there be two urns; that in each constituency a herald proclaim that whoever thinks the Generals did wrong in failing to rescue those who won the victory in the naval battle shall cast his vote in the first urn and whoever does not think so shall cast his vote in the second urn; and that, if it be decided that they did wrong, they be punished with death and handed over to the Eleven [5] and their property be confiscated, and a tenth thereof belong to the Goddess (*Athena*).'

Then a man came forward and said that he had been saved by clinging to a flour barrel and that those who were drowning told him, if he were saved, to report to the People that the Generals had failed to rescue those who had fought most gallantly for their fatherland.

Next a summons was served on Kallixenos for having made an illegal proposal; Euryptolemos son of Peisianax and a few others were the sponsors of it. Some of the People showed their approval of this, but the great mass shouted out that it was monstrous if the People were not allowed to do whatever they wished. Lykiskos took up this theme and proposed that, unless the summons be withdrawn, those who had served it should be judged by the same vote as the Generals; and as the mob broke out again in shouts of approval, they were forced to withdraw the summons.

Then some members of the Presiding Committee declared that they would not put the motion to the vote, since it was illegal. At this Kallixenos again mounted the platform and made the same complaint against them as had been made against Euryptolemos, and the crowd shouted that if they refused to put the motion to the vote they should be prosecuted. This terrified the members of the Committee, and all of them agreed to put the motion, except Socrates the son of Sophroniskos; Socrates said that he would do nothing at all that was contrary to law.

Euryptolemos then rose and spoke as follows in defence of the Generals:

'I have come to the platform, men of Athens, partly to accuse Perikles, although he is my kinsman and dear to me, and Diomedon, although he is a friend of mine, partly to speak in their defence, partly to recommend the measures that seem to be in the best interests of the community at large ... The course of action that I recommend is one that will make it impossible for you to be misled, either by me or by anyone else, and will enable you to act with full knowledge, in punishing those who have acted wrongly, and to inflict on them, collectively and individually, whatever punishment you please. What I propose is that you should allow them at least one day, if not more, to speak in their own defence, so that you will be relying on your own judgement rather than that of others. You all know, men of Athens, that the decree of Kannonos is extremely severe: it prescribes that anyone who has wronged the Athenian people should plead his case before the People after having been taken into custody, and, if he is found guilty, should be put to death and be thrown into the Pit, and should forfeit his property, a tenth of it being given to the Goddess. This is the decree under which I urge you to try the Generals, and to try Perikles, my kinsman, first, if you see fit; for it would be disgracefu for me to care more about him than about the community as a whole. Or, if you prefer, try them under the law applying to those charged with temple-robbery or treason, which prescribes that anyone who has betrayed the community or has stolen sacred property should be tried in a law court, and, if found guilty, be refused burial in Attica, his property being forfeit. Give these men a legal trial, men of Athens, under whichever of these laws you choose: a separate trial for each of them. If this procedure is followed, those who have done wrong will suffer the extreme penalty and those who are blameless will be set free, men of Athens, by your decision; men who have done no wrong will not be put to death. You will be observing the dictates of piety and the terms of your oath in giving them a legal trial; you will not be fighting on the side of the Lakedaimonians in putting to death without trial, in violation of the law, those who have gained a victory and have deprived the enemy of seventy ships. What are you afraid of, that makes you want to act in such excessive haste? Do you imagine that you will not be able to put to death or to set free anyone you please if you try them in accordance with the law, but that you will be able to do so if you settle the matter in violation of the law, in the way that Kallixenos has persuaded the Council to propose to the People, that is, by a single vote? But then you may put to death someone who is blameless, and later you will repent of it . . .'

After making this speech, he put forward a motion that the men should be tried in accordance with the decree of Kannonos, each of them separately: the Council's motion was that judgement should be passed on all of them together by a single vote. When there was a show of hands to decide between the two motions, they decided at first in favour of Euryptolemos' proposal, but when Menekles put in an objection under oath (*alleging illegality*), there was a fresh vote, and this time the Council's proposal was approved. They then voted on the eight Generals who had taken part in the battle. The vote went against them, and the six who were in Athens were put to death.

Not long afterwards the Athenians repented and voted that preliminary plaints be lodged against those who had deceived the People, that they furnish sureties until they come up for trial, and that Kallixenos be included among them. Plaints were lodged against four others also and they were taken into custody by their sureties, but later, during a civil disturbance, they escaped, before being brought to trial. Kallixenos returned at the time when the men of the Peiraieus[6] returned to the city, but everyone loathed him, and he died of starvation.

THE MACHINERY OF POPULAR RULE

Eighty years or so after this episode, Aristotle (or, as some think, one of his pupils) wrote an account of the development of the democratic system at Athens and of its main elements in his time. There had not been any fundamental change in the intervening years; the following excerpts from the second part of this account thus throw light on arrangements with which Xenophon expected his audience to be familiar.

Aristotle, *Constitution of Athens*

42. The political system is now organized as follows. The right to participate belongs to those who are of citizen birth on both sides.[7] They are entered on the rolls of the demes [8] at the age of eighteen.

When young men come up for enrolment, the members of the deme, after swearing an oath, decide by ballot, first whether they appear to have attained the age prescribed by law—if not, they go back among the boys, secondly whether the candidate is free and of such parentage as the laws require. If they reject him as not being free, he then asks for the matter to be referred to the Court of Justice,[9] and the members of the deme select five men from among themselves to put the case against him. If it is decided that he had no right to be enrolled, the state sells him;[10] but if he wins, the members are obliged to enrol him.

After this the Council inspects those who have been enrolled, and if any appears to be less than eighteen years old, it fines the members who enrolled him . . .

43. All the ordinary administrative offices are filled by lot, with the exception of three, those of Treasurer of the Military Fund, Treasurer of the Festival Fund and Superintendent of the Water Supply. These officials are elected by show of hands . . .[11] All military officers also are elected by show of hands.

The Council is appointed by lot. It consists of five hundred members, fifty from each constituency. The members from each of the constituencies take it in turns to act as the Presiding Committee, in an order determined by lot, the first four acting for thirty-six days each, the remaining six for thirty-five days each, since the reckoning is by lunar years.

The Presiding Committee messes together in the Tholos;[12] it receives money for this from public funds. It convokes the Council and the Assembly: the Council every day, with the exception of holidays, the Assembly of the People four times during the Committee's term of office. It puts up notices of the Council's agenda, the order of business for each day, and the place of meeting. It also puts up notices for meetings of the Assembly.[13] During each Committee's term of office there is one principal meeting, at which the People have to confirm the tenure of all holders of office, if they appear to be performing their duties properly, and to deal with the grain supply and the defence of the country. On this day, too, those who wish to introduce impeachments may do so,[14] and the inventories of confiscated property are read out, and also claims to succeed to property and to marry an heiress, so that nobody may miss the opportunity of entering a counter-claim.

During the sixth Committee's term, in addition to the business already mentioned, the Committee holds a vote by show of hands on whether or not to hold an ostracism;[15] also on preliminary plaints against malicious prosecutors, Athenians or resident aliens—up to three in either category—and on plaints alleging that an individual who has made a promise to the People has failed to perform it.

Another meeting in each Committee's term is for petitions. At this meeting anyone who wishes may place on the altar a suppliant's token and may then address the People on any matter, private or public.

The two remaining meetings in each term are concerned with all other business. The laws require that three of the items shall relate to religion, three to heralds and envoys, and three to secular matters . . .
44. The Presiding Committee has a Chairman, chosen by lot, who holds the Chairmanship for a day and a night; he may not hold it for longer, nor may the same man hold it twice. This man has charge of the keys of the sanctuaries in which the public records and funds are kept, and of the public seal. He is obliged to remain in the Tholos, together with one third of the Committee, chosen by himself. When the Committee convokes the Council or the Assembly, he appoints by lot,

from among the Councillors, nine Stewards, one from each constituency except the one to which the Committee belongs, and out of these nine one Chairman. To these Stewards he hands over the agenda.

Having received the agenda, the Stewards attend to the orderly conduct of the meeting, bring forward the items that have to be dealt with, act as tellers, and generally direct the proceedings. They also have authority to dismiss the meeting. No one may be Chairman more than once during the year, but a man may serve as Steward once during each Presiding Committee's term of office . . .[16]

45. In earlier times the Council had authority to inflict fines and sentences of imprisonment and of death . . . but the People later passed a law to the effect that, if the Council passes sentence on a person for an offence or imposes a penalty, the Thesmothetai have to bring the sentence or penalty before the Court of Justice, and the decision of the jurors is final.

Thus, for instance, although the Council investigates the conduct of most office-holders, especially those who handle money, its decisions are not final, but must be referred to the Court of Justice. Private citizens also have the right to lay information before the Council against any holder of office for failing to observe the laws, but here too there must be reference to the Court if the Council finds the charge proved.

Again, the Council examines those who are to be Councillors in the following year, and the nine Archons. In earlier times it had power to reject them, but now there must be reference to the Court in such cases.

In these matters, then, the Council does not have final authority.

It also holds a preliminary debate on matters brought before the People in Assembly. The People do not have the right to vote on anything unless it has been discussed beforehand by the Council and placed on the agenda by the Presiding Committee. Anyone who carries a motion which has not been discussed beforehand is liable to indictment for having broken the law.

(Aristotle goes on to describe various branches of the administration. One thing that emerges is the close control over all holders of office which the People exercised, through the Council of Five Hundred and the Courts.)

48. The Councillors choose ten Auditors by lot from among their own members to audit the accounts of the holders of office once in each of the year's ten terms.

They also choose by lot ten Examiners, one from each constituency, and two Assessors for each Examiner, who are required to sit during market hours beside the statue of the Hero after whom their constituency is named.[17] If anyone wishes to prefer a charge, either of a private or of a public nature, against any holder of office who has already undergone examination after his term of office in a Court of Justice, he must write on a whitewashed tablet, within three days after that examination, his own name, the name of the accused, the alleged offence and the penalty which he thinks appropriate and hand it to the Examiner. He takes it and considers it, and if he accepts the charge he refers it, if of a private nature, to the Deme Judges [18] responsible for bringing to court charges against those belonging to that constituency; if it is of a public nature, he hands in a written report to the Thesmothetai. If they accept the charge, they reopen the official's examination before the Court of Justice, and the jurors' decision is final . . .

54. Among the office-holders chosen by lot . . . there are ten Auditors and ten Assistant Auditors, to whom all those who have held an office are obliged to submit their accounts, for they alone audit the accounts of those who are accountable and submit the results of the audit to the Court of Justice. If they prove that someone has embezzled funds, the jurors find him guilty of embezzlement, and he repays ten times the amount in question. If they demonstrate that someone has taken bribes and the jurors find him guilty, they estimate the amount of the bribes and he likewise pays ten times this amount. If, however, they find him guilty of maladministration, they estimate the amount involved and he has to pay simply that amount, provided that he pays it in full before the ninth of the year's ten terms, otherwise the amount is doubled. (The tenfold payment is not doubled.) . . .

55. These office-holders, then, are chosen by lot, and are in charge of the business that I have mentioned.

Nowadays the Nine Archons, as they are called . . . , are also chosen by lot: six Thesmothetai, and their Clerk, the Archon, the Basileus, the Polemarchos: each from each of the constituencies in turn.[19]

They undergo an examination in the Council of Five Hundred, except the Clerk; he is examined only before a Court of Justice, like other office-holders (all of whom, whether chosen by lot or elected by show of hands, undergo an examination before entering on office), whereas the Nine Archons are examined in the Council and then again in a Court of Justice. In earlier times a man whom the Council rejected did not take up office, but now a rejection is referred to the Court of Justice, and its decision is final.

When a man is examined, the first questions he is asked are: 'Who is your father? Of which deme? Who was his father? Who is your mother? Who was her father? Of which deme?' Then they ask him if he has an ancestral Apollo and a household Zeus, and where their shrines are,[20] and next whether he has family tombs, and where they are, and finally whether he treats his parents well, and to what property class he belongs,[21] and whether he has served on the military campaigns. After being asked these questions, he is told, 'Call your witnesses'. When he has presented his witnesses, the presiding officer asks, 'Who wishes to prefer a charge against this man?', and if someone comes forward, time is given to hear the charge and the reply, and a vote is then taken, in the Council by show of hands, in the Court by ballot. If no one wishes to prefer a charge, the ballot is held forthwith. In earlier days one man cast his ballot in such cases, but nowadays they are all obliged to cast their ballots, the object being that, if some scoundrel has got rid of his accusers, the jurors have the power to reject him.

After being examined in this way, they proceed to the stone on which the portions of sacrificial victims have been placed . . . , and stepping on to it they swear to carry out their duties justly and in accordance with the laws, and not to accept gifts in connection with their duties, and to dedicate a golden statue if they accept a gift. After swearing, they proceed to the Akropolis and swear the same oath again there, and then they enter on their office . . .

62. Fees are given as follows. First, a man receives a drachma for attendance at ordinary meetings of the Assembly, and nine obols at the principal meetings. Secondly, the jurors in the Courts of Justice receive three obols. Thirdly, the Council receives five obols, and an additional obol is given to members of the Presiding Committee as a maintenance allowance . . .[22] (*Aristotle goes on to mention the fees paid to the Archons and to certain office-holders: but his list is selective, not complete. We do not know how many officials were paid, or how much, or since when, or for how long after his time the payment of officials was maintained.*)

The military offices may be held repeatedly;[23] but none of the others may be held more than once, except that a man may be a Councillor twice.

63. The selection by lot of jurors for the Courts of Justice is conducted by the nine Archons, each selecting from one constituency, with the Clerk to the Thesmothetai conducting the selection from the tenth constituency ... (*Aristotle proceeds to describe the machinery that they used.*) All who are over thirty years of age may serve as jurors, provided that they are not debtors to the state and have not been deprived of their civic rights ... (*He goes on to describe the empanelling of juries for trials. This last part of the papyrus is very fragmentary.*) In most of the Courts there are five hundred jurors ... but when necessary ... two panels sit together ... and some cases are heard before one thousand five hundred jurors, that is, three panels ...[24] (*He goes on to describe the procedure for voting after a case has been heard.*) Whichever party receives the greater number of votes is the winner, but if the number is equal the defendant wins ...

ORATORY AND LEADERSHIP

The following passages illustrate further how democracy worked at Athens during the period of slightly more than a hundred years, from the death of Perikles in 429 to the death of Aristotle in 322, from which we have the most evidence.

First, a picture, by Demosthenes, in a speech delivered in 330, of the working of the system at a moment of crisis, in 338, when news reached Athens of the invasion of central Greece by King Philip of Macedon, who was trying to bring all the little republics of European Greece under his control.

Demosthenes, *On the Crown* 169–170

It was evening. Someone came to bring the Presiding Committee the news that Elatea had fallen. They at once got up in the middle of their dinner, turned out the occupants of the stalls in the Agora, and set light to the wickerwork screens,[25] while others went to fetch the Generals and summoned the trumpeter. Soon the whole city was in an uproar.

The following day, at dawn, the Presiding Committee summoned the Council to the Council House, while you, gentlemen, made your way to the Assembly; and before the Council had discussed the situation and prepared a motion, the whole citizen body was seated on the Pnyx.[26] Then, after the Council had arrived and the Presiding Committee had reported the news that they had received and the bearer of the news had been brought forward and had spoken, the herald asked: 'Who wishes to speak?' No one came forward. The herald kept repeating his question, but still no one rose to his feet, although all the Generals were present, and so were all the usual speakers, and the fatherland was calling for someone to make proposals for its salvation: for when the herald speaks as the law requires, it is right to regard his voice as the voice of the fatherland.

More light is thrown on the working of the Assembly by the following passage from a speech which Aischines, who was active as a public speaker during the same period as Demosthenes, often in opposition to him, delivered in a Court of Justice as prosecutor of Timarchos, an ally of Demosthenes. Timarchos, Aischines alleged, had been a prostitute in his youth.

Aischines, *Against Timarchos* 27–32

The law has explicitly specified who may and who may not speak in the Assembly. It does not disqualify a man who has no Generals among his ancestors, or who follows some trade in order to provide himself with his daily bread. On the contrary, it welcomes such men. That is why the herald is required to ask repeatedly, 'Who wishes to speak?'

Whom, then does the law forbid to speak? Those whose lives have been disgraceful: they are not allowed to speak in the Assembly. Where is this laid down? I will quote the text of the Examination of Public Speakers: 'The following may not speak in the Assembly. Anyone who strikes his father or his mother, or fails to provide either his father or his mother with board and lodging ... Anyone who has failed to serve on campaigns on which he was ordered to serve, or has thrown away his shield ... Anyone who has been a prostitute or has cohabited with a man for reward ... Anyone who has squandered property which has fallen to him as heir, whether from his parents or from another source ...'

If anyone speaks in contravention of these rules, the law lays down that 'any Athenian who wishes and is entitled to do so may demand an investigation'.[27] And you, the citizens of Athens, are required to investigate the matter in Court. This law was passed long ago . . .

Gorgias, a native of the Greek state Leontinoi in Sicily, whose views Plato is purporting to express in the following passage from the dialogue known by his name, was one of the first men to offer systematic instruction in the art of persuading an audience. His first visit to Athens was in 427. As a modern commentator on this dialogue has said, it would appear 'that Gorgias is here exaggerating a good deal . . . But there is nevertheless an important kernel of truth in Gorgias' claim: in the conditions of Greek democracy a skilful orator could certainly on occasion exert a disproportionate and dangerous influence.'*

Plato, *Gorgias* 455–459

Gorgias. You know, of course, that the dockyards and the fortifications of Athens and the port installations were constructed on the advice of Themistokles and, in part, Perikles, not on that of the specialists.
Socrates. That is what we are told about Themistokles, Gorgias. As for Perikles, I myself heard him recommend the building of the middle wall.[28]
Gorgias. And whenever a decision has to be made on matters such as you mentioned just now, you can see that those who act as advisers and those who get their proposals adopted are the regular public speakers . . . I maintain that if, in any state you like, a doctor and a trained speaker had to compete in the Assembly or before some other large audience to determine which should be given an appointment as a medical officer, the doctor would be nowhere; the man with ability as a speaker would get the job if he wanted it . . .
Socrates. And you say that you can make a speaker of anyone who is willing to learn from you?
Gorgias. Yes.
Socrates. Whatever the subject matter, he will be able to win over a mass audience, not by instructing them but by persuading them?
Gorgias. Certainly.

* E. R. Dodds, *Plato: Gorgias* (1959), 209.

Socrates. You were saying just now that even on matters of health the public speaker will be more convincing than the doctor.
Gorgias. Yes, that is what I was saying—at least where a mass audience is concerned.
Socrates. Well now, a mass audience means an ignorant audience, doesn't it? Surely he won't be more convincing than the doctor before an expert audience.
Gorgias. You are right.
Socrates. So the art of public speaking doesn't depend on knowing the truth about things; it depends on having discovered a technique of persuasion, so that one can give the ignorant the impression that one knows more than the experts.
Gorgias. Well, isn't it a great comfort, Socrates, to be able to get the better of specialists without having acquired any skills other than this?

Xenophon, a contemporary of Plato, also wrote dialogues in which Socrates figures as protagonist, one set of them being known as *Memoirs*. Whether they give us a more or a less misleading portrait of Socrates, they too throw light on the working of democracy.

Xenophon, *Memoirs* 3.7

When Socrates saw that, although Glaukon's son, Charmides,[29] was a man of note and much abler than those who were then active in politics, he shrank from coming before the People and taking a hand in public affairs, he said: 'Tell me, Charmides, supposing that there was somebody who was capable of winning athletic contests and thus gaining honour for himself and enhancing his country's reputation in the Greek world, but who refused to compete, what sort of man would you think he was?'

'Obviously, soft and cowardly,' Charmides replied.

'And supposing that there was somebody who was capable of taking a hand in public affairs and thus raising his country's prestige and gaining honour for himself, but shrank from doing so, would it not be natural to regard him, too, as cowardly?'

'Perhaps,' he said, 'but why ask me?'

'Because I think that although you are a man of ability you shrink from taking a hand in affairs in which as a citizen you are under an obligation to participate.'

'I a man of ability?' said Charmides. 'In what activities of mine have you seen evidence that leads you to make this accusation?'

'In your conversations with politicians. When they consult you on anything, I notice that you give them good advice, and when they make some mistake, you offer sound criticism.'

'A private discussion, Socrates,' he said, 'is not the same thing as a public debate.'

'But surely a man who knows how to count can count just as well in public as by himself, and those who are best at playing the lyre when they are on their own are those who also excel before an audience.'

'You are forgetting about shyness and stage-fright,' he replied. 'Don't you realize that these are part of human nature, and that one experiences them much more intensely in public assemblies than in private gatherings?'

'Yes, and I have had it in mind to point something out to you. You are not shy with highly intelligent people, and you are not frightened of extremely influential people, yet you are too modest to speak in front of the silliest and the most insignificant. Are you overcome with modesty in the presence of fullers and shoemakers and joiners and smiths and farmers and merchants and market traders . . .? They are the people of whom the Assembly is composed . . . So don't neglect public affairs, if you can make some contribution to improving things; for if things go well, it is not only the citizen body at large that will reap the benefit—so will your personal friends, and not least yourself.'

In his old age, Aristophanes (c. 452–385), who had been presenting Athenian audiences with comedies, mostly with a strong element of political satire, since 427, wrote a play (which was produced in 392, or thereabouts), about what might happen if women took control of public life. The women have begun by disguising themselves in men's clothes and packing the Assembly (which as women they had no right to attend).

Aristophanes, *Women in Assembly* 376–461

Blepyros. But where have you come from?
Chremes. From the Assembly.

Blepyros. Meaning that the meeting is over already?
Chremes. Yes, it was over by bloody dawn . . .
Blepyros. But you got your three obols?
Chremes. If only I had. But I arrived too late.
Blepyros. But why was that?
Chremes. A terrific crowd, I've never seen anything like it, all going to the Pnyx. And they all looked like shoemakers. In the Assembly it was like a sea of white faces.[30] Extraordinary. So I didn't get my fee, nor did a lot of others.
Blepyros. That means I wouldn't get anything if I went now?
Chremes. How could you? You wouldn't have done if you'd gone as soon as the cock had crowed twice.
Blepyros (misquoting Aischylos). 'O, what a poor wretch am I. Weep not for the three obols, Antilochos, weep for me, who have to live on without them. All that was mine is lost.' But what was on the agenda to draw such an enormous crowd so early?
Chremes. What was on the agenda? The Presiding Committee had decided to have a debate on the safety of the Republic. And at the very first moment that bleary-eyed Neokleides sneaked on to the platform. The people howled—you can imagine. 'It's a scandal, him speaking in public, especially when it's a question of our safety. He couldn't save his own eyelashes.' Well, he looked round the crowd and bawled out: 'What, I ask you, ought I to do?'
Blepyros. 'Pound together an onion and some asafoetida, add some Lakonian spurge, and rub it on your eyelids last thing at night.' That's what I'd have said if I'd been there.
Chremes. The next speaker was that crafty bloke Euaion. He came on to the platform in shirtsleeves, or so it seemed to most of us, but he insisted that he was wearing a cloak. Then he launched into a real vote-catching speech. 'You see before you a man who is himself in dire need of a saviour. Ten pounds would do the trick. All the same, I can tell you how to ensure the safety of the Republic and the citizens. If the fullers give woollen cloaks to all who need them, as soon as the sun begins to sink, none of us will ever catch pleurisy. Anyone who hasn't got a bed or bedding should have the right to go along after his bath to the tanneries and sleep there; anyone who closes the door on him in winter should pay a fine of three hides.'
Blepyros. That was damned good advice. He only needed to add one thing and nobody would have voted against him: the grain merchants

should make the poor a present of three bushels for their dinner—or else. Nausikydes could have done some good for once.
Chremes. Next, a good-looking lad with a pale complexion jumped up to make a speech—he looked like Nikias. He began saying that the government should be handed over to the women. Then people began stamping their feet and shouting 'Hear, hear!'—at least, the crowd of shoemakers did, but the country folk began muttering.
Blepyros. They had some bloody sense.
Chremes. But they were a minority. And he managed to shout them down, with his praise of women and his abuse of you.
Blepyros. Well, what did he say?
Chremes. First, he said that you're a rogue . . .
Blepyros. What about you?
Chremes. That wasn't all. A thief as well.
Blepyros. Only me?
Chremes. And a bloody blackmailer into the bargain.
Blepyros. Still only me?
Chremes (*pointing to the audience*). No, all that bloody crowd as well.
Blepyros. But who says otherwise?
Chremes. A woman, he says, is a creature with some sense. She has a head for business. And she isn't always blabbing secrets about women's religious rites, he says, which is the sort of thing we do, you and I, when we're Councillors.
Blepyros. Aye, that's the bloody truth.
Chremes. Then they lend each other things, he says: clothes, jewellery, silver, cups, woman to woman, without calling in witnesses; and they give them all back: they don't rob one another. That's what most of *us* do, or so he said.
Blepyros. We bloody well do, and with witnesses.
Chremes. They don't inform against each other, they don't take each other to court, they don't try to deprive the People of their rights. Those were some of his reasons for singing women's praises.
Blepyros. So what was decided?
Chremes. To hand over the government to them, since that seemed to be the only thing we haven't tried, so far as government is concerned.
Blepyros. And the motion was passed?
Chremes. That's what I'm telling you.
Blepyros. And they've been given all the chores that we citizens used to tackle?

Chremes. That's how things are.
Blepyros. So I shan't go to sit in Court? It'll be the wife?
Chremes. And you won't have to feed your brats. It'll be the wife.
Blepyros. And I shan't be the one who groans as each day dawns?
Chremes. No, thank god, that'll be another job for the women. You can stay at home farting, without a care on your mind.
Blepyros. There's one risk, all the same, for men of our age. When they've taken over the reins of government, they may force us—
Chremes. To do what?
Blepyros. To screw them.
Chremes. What if we can't?
Blepyros. They won't give us any lunch.
Chremes. You'd better pull yourself together, man, so you won't miss out on either.
Blepyros. But it's dreadful to be forced to do it.
Chremes. But if it's for the country's good, every man must do his duty.
Blepyros. Well, there's a saying among the old folk, that, however daft our schemes are, things always work out all right for us in the end.

POPULAR SOVEREIGNTY AND THE RULE OF LAW

Aristophanes imagines the assembled People deciding by a single vote to hand over to the women of Athens complete control of the community. This was fantasy, but fantasy that had its roots in painful memories. In 411 the assembled People, influenced partly by false promises, partly by terrorism organized by a group of conspirators, decided by a single show of hands to give autocratic power to a body of Four Hundred, dominated by the conspirators; in 404, under pressure from the victorious Spartans, they decided by a single show of hands to give autocratic power to a body of Thirty.

These were extreme instances of the dangers inherent in conferring unfettered sovereignty on the Assembly. But even in more normal circumstances, if the People, or rather those of the People who have opportunity, means and inclination to spend several hours at a meeting of the Assembly, have complete freedom to enact by a majority vote decrees binding on the whole community, laying down, not only what should be done about sending envoys to Delphi the following week but what should be done about such and such whenever such and such occurs, and if those of them who assemble a month later enact quite different and even conflicting decrees, how can orderly communal life continue?

In a passage from his *Memoirs*, quoted below, in chapter IV, Xenophon reports what Perikles was supposed to have said on this subject in a private conversation towards the end of his life, before the precariousness of such a system had become obvious.

It was through making practical experiments, not through philosophical debate, that the People found solutions to the problem of reconciling the demand for popular sovereignty with the desire for a stable constitutional framework within which people would know what to expect. The first step was taken probably not long after the death of Perikles in 429, certainly before 415. It was made permissible for any citizen to enter an indictment (called a *graphe paranomon*, that is to say, a written statement specifying illegalities) against any degree or any proposed decree which, in his view, conflicted, in its content or formally, with some existing law, and (if it was less than a year old) against its proposer. A sworn statement of one's intention to enter such an indictment sufficed to suspend the operation of a decree or the voting on a proposal pending trial. If a popular Court sustained the objection, the proposal lapsed; if it had already been passed, it was quashed.

It is significant that in 411 the People were induced to revoke this safeguard before the proposal to give power to the Four Hundred was voted on; this shows both its importance and its inadequacy. But in other respects also the state of affairs remained unsatisfactory. By no means everything which the People decreed could properly be regarded as a law and, as such, in need of protection against a sudden change of mind; but some of its decrees certainly had the scope of laws; indeed, it was only as decrees that laws could be brought into being. How was one to distinguish between what was a law and what was not? Moreover there were gaps and inconsistencies in the accumulated body of enactments that could be called laws, as the debate on the treatment of the Generals in 406 shows; it is doubtful whether their trial was, strictly speaking, illegal.

Serious efforts to meet these difficulties had been initiated a few years previously, not long after the ousting of the Four Hundred. For one thing, a commission was established to collect all enactments that might properly be called laws. Its activity was interrupted by the coming to power of the Thirty in 404 but was immediately resumed when democracy was restored in 403; and steps were also then taken to fill gaps and to remove inconsistencies and obsolete details. Moreover machinery was created, for future use, for the repeal and amendment of laws and for the creation of new laws; machinery which was more slow-moving, and hedged about with greater safeguards, than machinery for the passing of decrees. 'It was not a question of the sovereign people allowing itself to be robbed of full control of the law-making machine; it deliberately invented a perfectly democratic brake to slow down the machine.' *

Andokides, a member of an old noble family who had been in trouble for sacrilege in his youth, referred to some of these developments in a speech that he made in court in 399, pleading for his rehabilitation. He reminds the court of their actions after the ousting of the junta in 403.

Andokides, *On the Mysteries* 82–87

You held an Assembly at which you considered the state of the laws, and you decreed that, after all the laws had been examined, those of them that were ratified should be engraved in the Portico.[31] (*To the Clerk*) Read out the decree . . .

(*This decree made provision also for review and amendment, allowing for proposals from any citizen, and for final examination by the Council and by a Legislative Commission of five hundred, elected in the demes, no doubt in proportion to their population.*)

So the laws were examined, gentlemen, in accordance with this decree, and those which were ratified were engraved on the walls of the Portico. When the engraving was complete, we passed a law which all of you observe. (*To the Clerk*) Read out the law.

'In no circumstances whatsoever may the authorities apply an unwritten law . . .' (*Andokides goes on to have extracts from other laws read out.*) 'No decree, whether of the Council or of the People, may override a law . . . No law applying to an individual may be passed, if it does not apply equally to all Athenians, unless six thousand votes have been cast in favour by secret ballot.'

Probably not long after the passing of these measures, a further step was taken to discourage ill-considered attempts to alter laws: it was made permissible for any citizen to enter an indictment against anyone who had proposed, or had succeeded in enacting, a law detrimental to the Athenian people. In 353 Demosthenes brought a charge of this nature against Timokrates, the author of a law dealing with the payment of debts to the

* A. R. W. Harrison, *Journal of Hellenic Studies* 75 (1955), 35.

Treasury, which, according to Demosthenes, had been submitted without previous publicity to a legislative commission set up for a different purpose.

Demosthenes, *Against Timokrates*

19. I shall begin by describing the first of Timokrates' crimes, his legislating in contravention of every law ... (*To the Clerk of the Court*) Please take these laws and read them out. It will become apparent that he did none of the things which they require. Pay attention, gentlemen, to the laws as they are read out.

20. 'On the eleventh day of each year, at the Assembly held on that day, after the herald has said the prayers, votes shall be taken on the laws by show of hands: first on those relating to the Council, secondly on those of general application, thirdly on those that concern the Nine Archons, lastly on those relating to other officers. The first to vote shall be those who consider that the laws relating to the Council are satisfactory, the next, those who consider that they are not; similarly in the case of the laws of general application ...

21. If the voting goes against any group of the established laws, the Presiding Committee under whose presidency the voting takes place shall put the question of these laws on the agenda for the last of the three forthcoming meetings of the Assembly. The Stewards who happen to be on duty at that meeting shall be obliged to bring forward, immediately after the sacrifices, the question of a Legislative Committee—arrangements for its sittings and for the payment of its members. The members shall be drawn from among those who have sworn the Court Oath (*i.e. from the list of those qualified to serve as jurors; such committees had typically 501 or 1001 members*) ...

23. 'Prior to the meeting of the Assembly, any Athenian who wishes to submit proposals for new laws shall put these in writing and display them in front of the statues of the Eponymous Heroes, so that the People can take the volume of proposals into account in fixing the duration of the sittings of the Committee.

'The proposer of a new law shall write it out on a whitewashed board and display it in front of the Eponymous Heroes every day until the Assembly meets.

'To state the case for the laws which the Committee is to be asked to repeal, the People shall elect five men from among all Athenians on the eleventh day of Hekatombaion.' [32]

24. All these laws have been in force for a long time, gentlemen (*in fact, some fifty years*), and experience has shown again and again that they are in your interests. No-one has ever uttered a word against them: which is not surprising, for there is nothing harsh or compulsive or oligarchic in their provisions; on the contrary, the procedure which they prescribe is thoroughly beneficent and serves the people's interests . . .

32. But Timokrates' complete disregard of these provisions is only one part of his crime: I shall now demonstrate to you in detail that the law he brought in is in conflict with all existing laws. (*To the Clerk*) Take first, please, this law, which expressly forbids the submission of a legislative proposal that is in conflict with an existing law, and orders the indictment of anyone who submits such a proposal. Read it out.

33. 'No established law may be repealed, save in a Legislative Committee. There any Athenian who wishes may move the repeal of a law, provided that he proposes another in its stead. To choose between them, the Stewards shall organize voting by show of hands, first on whether or not the established law serves the interests of the Athenian people, and then on the proposed law. Whichever of the two the Committee approves by show of hands shall be binding.

'No law may be in conflict with any established law.

'If anyone in moving the repeal of one of the established laws proposes in its stead a law which does not serve the interests of the Athenian people, or is in conflict with some other established law, he may be indicted under the law that deals with the proposing of detrimental laws.'

34. You have heard the law. Among the many good laws that exist in our state, it is, I believe, as commendably drafted as any. Notice how fair it is and how strongly in the People's interests . . .

37. For the only just and reliable way of protecting the laws is to give responsibility to you, gentlemen of the jury, numerous as you are: for no-one can deprive you of your ability to discern what is best before giving your sanction; no-one can get you out of the way or corruptly procure your consent to the replacement of a good law by one that is inferior . . .

(*Demosthenes goes on, first to demonstrate that Timokrates' law is in conflict with existing laws; secondly, to argue that it is detrimental to the Athenian People, inter alia because it annuls decisions of the Courts.*)

138. Do not allow yourselves or the state to be treated in this outrageous fashion. Remember that not long ago, in the archonship of Evandros,[33] when Eudemos of Kydathenai was found guilty of having proposed a detrimental law, you condemned him to death; and Philippos, son of Philippos the shipowner, only barely escaped the death penalty, because he made the counterproposal of a huge fine and you accepted his proposal by a small majority. Treat this man now with the same indignation . . .

152. If someone, by bringing in a new law, can annul decisions that have been reached in Court by the juror's vote, where will it end? . . .

153. A man who does this is pointing the way for others to the dissolution of our Courts of Justice and the recall of men who have been banished and other terrible things of that sort . . .

154. I have heard that this was how our democracy was destroyed in the past: the first steps were to put an end to the indictment of illegal proposals and to annul decisions of the Courts . . .

CITIZENS AND OUTSIDERS

The two speeches for the prosecution in a lawsuit in about 340 likewise illustrate the awareness of the Athenians in the fourth century that, for the health of democracy, respect for the People's will must be reconciled with respect for the law. That they were aware of this is surely as significant as that they were not wholly successful in achieving it. The complaint of Aristotle, echoed later by Cicero, amongst others, that democracy often meant government by popular decree, to the neglect of law, suggests that many other democratic states were less successful.

These two speeches (which are not by Demosthenes, but somehow came to be included in antiquity in collected editions of his works) illustrate also the exclusiveness of the Athenian citizen body. A family could be resident at Athens for generations without acquiring citizenship, and therewith not only the right to intermarry with Athenians but even the right to own land or a house. An alien could obtain these rights only by decree of the People, and only as a reward for services to the community. Generally speaking, democratic states were as exclusive as any in their attitude to outsiders, Greek and non-Greek alike, once they were firmly established, although according to Aristotle they tended to be much more liberal in early days, when the aim was to strengthen the commons over against the old ruling class (see below, chapter III, on Kleisthenes at Athens).

The defendant is a woman named Neaira. The charge against her is that, although she is an alien, she has married an Athenian citizen, Stephanos, and has borne him children who have been passed off as being of citizen birth. Theomnestos, the prosecutor, begins by explaining his personal grievances against Stephanos, which have led him to retaliate by prosecuting Neaira.

[Demosthenes], *Against Neaira*

2. . . . The Athenian People had decreed that Pasion and his descendants should be Athenians, in recognition of his services to the community.[34] My father approved of this award, and gave Pasion's son, Apollodoros, his daughter's—my sister's—hand in marriage; she is the mother of Apollodoros' children . . .

3. Some time later, it fell to Apollodoros' lot to serve as a Councillor. After he had passed his test and sworn the prescribed oath, war broke out and the situation became critical . . .

4. Apollodoros, in his capacity as Councillor, put through Council and brought before the People a decree which prescribed that the People should vote by show of hands to determine whether any funds that were left over after administrative needs had been met should be earmarked for military purposes or for festival purposes. The laws do in fact prescribe that in time of war any such surplus should be earmarked for military purposes; but Apollodoros thought that the People ought to be free to decide what they wished to do with their own property, and he had taken an oath to act as Councillor in the best interests of the Athenian People.

5. When the determining vote was taken, no one opposed the use of the money in question for military purposes . . . But Stephanos here challenged the legality of Apollodoros' decree, and when the matter came to Court . . . the decree was quashed.

6. As to Stephanos having seen fit to bring this about, we do not complain; but when the jury came to voting on the penalty,[35] he refused to make any concession in response to our pleas and proposed a fine of fifteen talents, with the object of depriving Apollodoros and his sons of their civic rights and reducing my sister and all of us to

utter helplessness and complete destitution. (7) For Apollodoros' whole property did not amount to as much as three talents, so that it would have been impossible for him to pay so large a debt; but if the debt had not been paid within the ninth prytany it would have been doubled and Apollodoros would have been listed as owing the Treasury thirty talents; and once he had been registered with the Treasury all his property would have been listed as belonging to the state, it would have been auctioned off, and he and his children and his wife and all of us would have been reduced to utter helplessness.[36] (8) Moreover, his other daughter would inevitably have been left unmarried, for who would ever have taken her without a dowry, from a man in debt to the Treasury and bereft of resources?

Such are the misfortunes that Stephanos sought to bring down on us, although we had never done him any harm. However, I owe the jurors who tried the case my profound gratitude for having at least declined to let him be pillaged; they fined him a talent, which he was just able to pay.

One good turn deserves another, so we have endeavoured to give Stephanos as good as we got . . .

13. That is why I am here, to prove to you that he is cohabiting with a foreign woman in contravention of the law;[37] that he has foisted alien children on the members of his phratry[38] and his deme; that he has given the daughters of courtesans in marriage, passing them off as his own; that he has behaved impiously to the gods; and that he is depriving the People of their right to choose whom they will make a citizen . . .

(*Theomnestos, it will be noted, does not venture to suggest that Apollodoros deserved no punishment for having tried to let the People make decisions in defiance of the law, however praiseworthy his motives;* * *and when Apollodoros himself subsequently addresses the court in support of Theomnestos—whose short opening speech he had probably written for him—he presents himself as an ardent champion of the rule of law: showing what he believed the jurors' feelings on this subject were likely to be.*)

88. . . . The Athenian People, who have full control over all the community's affairs and who can do whatever they please, have viewed Athenian citizenship as such a fine and august privilege for anyone to acquire that they have passed laws which they themselves

---

* He perhaps wished to enable the Athenians in future to build up a military reserve in peacetime if they so desired.

are compelled to observe if they want to make anyone a citizen, laws which have been trampled on by Stephanos here and by those who have contracted similar marriages. (89) It will be to your advantage to be reminded of them; you will realize how shockingly the finest and most august privileges that the community can confer on benefactors have been debased.

First, there is a law in force that forbids the grant of citizenship to anyone who has not earned this award by distinguished service to the Athenian People. Secondly, when the People have been convinced and have made the grant, it cannot become effective unless it is put to the vote at the next meeting of the Assembly and more than six thousand Athenians cast their votes by secret ballot . . . (90) Finally, the law allows any Athenian who wishes to do so to prosecute a new citizen on a charge of illegality: he can go before a jury and prove that the man is not worthy of the award, that he has become an Athenian in contravention of the laws . . .

92. You see what good and strict citizenship laws we have, laws with which anyone becoming an Athenian must conform; but on top of all these there is another most important law in our code; it shows what care the People have taken, in their own interests and on behalf of the Gods, to ensure that the rules of piety are observed when sacrifices are made on behalf of the community. This law expressly prohibits those on whom the Athenian People have conferred citizenship from holding any of the nine Archonships or any priesthood whatsoever. Their descendants, however, have been accorded by the People a share in all rights, 'provided only that they are the issue of a woman who is a citizen and has been legally wed' . . .

114. Each one of you, in casting his vote, should bear in mind that he is casting it to protect his wife, or his daughter, or his mother, or the community, the law and religion: to save our women's reputations from being assimilated to the reputation of this harlot, to prevent the status and rights of those who have been reared by their menfolk with every proper care for decency, and have been given in legal marriage, from being rendered indistinguishable from those accorded to a woman who has had vile dealings several times a day with a series of men, to suit their various whims. (115) Do not think of yourselves as listening to Apollodoros, or to the citizens who will be speaking in Neaira's defence; bear in mind that the contest is between the laws and this woman and relates to the things that she has done. While it

is the prosecution's turn, lend your ears to the very laws by which this community is governed, in conformity with which you have sworn to reach your verdict, taking note of what they ordain and how they have been transgressed. When the turn comes for the defence, recall the legal basis of the indictment and the evidence that has been given in support of it, look into this woman's face and ask yourselves simply whether she, being Neaira, has done what is alleged . . .

ACCOUNTABILITY

The close control that the Athenians exercised over those who held office is one of the things that emerges most clearly from Aristotle's account of the political system. Some of the implications are emphasized by Aischines in the opening passages of the speech which he delivered in Court in 330 in prosecuting Ktesiphon for having proposed that the People should confer honours on Demosthenes at a moment when he had not yet undergone examination after the conclusion of his tenure of an office.

Aischines, *Against Ktesiphon*

9. Next I want to say a few words about the laws that deal with the accountability of office-holders, laws which Ktesiphon has transgressed in drafting this decree. In the past, some officials who held very important offices and were in charge of the revenues . . . were in the habit of forestalling the examination that they had to undergo by procuring votes of thanks and public commendations . . . (11) In view of this, someone brought in a law, an excellent law, which explicitly forbids the award of crowns to those who have still to undergo examination . . . (12) Ktesiphon, gentlemen, has transgressed the law on accountability by proposing to award a crown to Demosthenes in mid-term, before he has passed his audit or his examination.
13. My opponents, gentlemen, will claim that when someone has been elected to do something under the terms of a decree, that is not an office, but a sort of commission or service. They will maintain that offices are, first, those which the Thesmothetai fill by drawing lots at their meetings in the Temple of Theseus, and secondly those which the People fill regularly by show of hands at the elections (the offices of General, Cavalry Commander and suchlike), all the rest being

functions assigned under the terms of decrees. (14) My reply to these arguments is to quote the law which you yourselves passed with the object of eliminating such evasions. The law refers explicitly to 'the elective offices', comprehending all of them in this one term, and adding that all positions which the People fill by show of hands are offices: 'and', it continues, 'the Inspector of Public Works'. Now Demosthenes was a Commissioner of Fortifications, inspector of the most important of such works. 'And all who are involved in public administration for more than thirty days. And all who assume the Presidency of Courts of Justice.' Now, every Inspector of Public Works may preside in a court. What are such persons instructed to do? Not to 'perform a service', but to 'hold office, after passing an examination in court' (for officials chosen by lot are likewise not exempt from examination; they too hold office after passing an examination). And they are instructed to 'submit their accounts and records in writing to the Auditors', like all other office-holders. To prove to you the correctness of what I have been saying, the Clerk of the Court will read out these laws . . .

17. . . . In this great and ancient community of ours, no one who has been involved in any way in public affairs is unaccountable. (18) I shall begin by giving you some surprising examples. For instance, priests and priestesses are by law accountable, all of them collectively and each individually . . . (19) Again, captains of warships are by law accountable . . . although it is recognized that they expend their inherited wealth in their eagerness to win honour in your sight . . . (20) Again, the Council of Five Hundred has been made accountable. (21) Moreover, the law is so mistrustful of those who are accountable that it states right at the outset that 'an officeholder who is accountable shall not go abroad'. Again, anyone who is accountable is forbidden to consecrate his property or make a dedication or let himself be adopted or devise his property by will, or anything of that kind. In a word, the law holds the property of those who are accountable as security until they submit accounts to the community.

JURORS AND PROSECUTORS

By now it will have become apparent how important a part in Athens' democratic government was played by the Courts of Justice, the Dikasteria, not only in dealing with crimes and misdemeanours and adjudicating in disputes between individuals, but also in protecting the laws (or, as we might say, the constitution), controlling holders of office and examining qualifications. Since it was impossible for the assembled People to attend to all of these matters, except in the gravest cases, the next best thing was to put them in the hands of a Court with several hundred members, selected at random by lot from a list of six thousand volunteers, as Aristotle describes. (A number of minor changes had been made in the system before his time, in the light of experience.) An official within whose sphere the matter for hearing fell presided in Court, but did not act as a judge. From the Court's decision there was no appeal. 'It says much for the Athenians' alertness and critical sense that the system worked as well as it did.' *

The fee which a juror received for a day spent in Court was much less than what a family needed for survival and what a man could earn by working. For many of the jurors it was something of the nature of an old-age pension.

Not all disputes or misdemeanours demanded the attention of several hundred citizens. Minor misdemeanours were dealt with summarily by the official or officials concerned. For disputes of many kinds between individuals there was a system of arbitration, citizens being required to serve individually as arbitrators during their sixtieth year, after they ceased to be liable for military service; such disputes came to Court only if arbitration failed.

In a play by Aristophanes, produced in 422—*Wasps* (so called because the chorus, of jurors, were dressed as wasps)—Philokleon ('friend of Kleon'), an elderly man passionately attached to jury service, is explaining its attractions to his son Bdelykleon ('loather of Kleon'), who wants to break him of the habit. At that time Kleon, a politician whom Aristophanes (like Thucydides) detested, was at the height of his influence, which he maintained, Aristophanes implies, by playing on the greed and fear of ordinary Athenians—fear, which he encouraged, that members of the old nobility were for ever plotting to subvert the democratic order.

Aristophanes, *Wasps* 548–691

Philokleon. Yes, I'll prove to you, right from the word 'go', that serving as a juror is as good as sitting on a king's throne. What creature is luckier or happier than a juror, more pampered, more formidable, even if he is an old man? To begin with, as soon as I get

* D. M. MacDowell, *Oxford Classical Dictionary* (second edition, 1970), s.v. *Dikasterion.*

up in the morning, great men, six feet tall, are looking out for me by the court enclosure. Then, as soon as I appear, someone puts his hand in mine—a smooth hand that has pinched some public money. People appeal to me, cringing and pouring out pitiful pleas: 'Have mercy on me, sir, I beg of you, if ever you yourself kept something back when you were in office or were buying food for your mess.' The fellow wouldn't have known me from Adam, if he hadn't been acquitted last time.

After listening to these requests and having my indignation mollified, I enter the Court; and, once inside, I do none of the things I've been promising. But I sit and listen to men talking as hard as they can to get themselves acquitted. What form of flattery is there, I wonder, that people don't try on jurors? Some moan about their poverty, and exaggerate their troubles, until each of them, as he goes on, has piled his up as high as—mine. Others spin yarns. Others tell us something amusing out of Aesop. Others crack jokes, trying to make me laugh and cool my temper. If none of these tricks work, a fellow gets hold of his children, his daughters and his sons, and drags them into Court. I listen to them bleating in chorus as they huddle there together. Then their father beseeches me in trembling tones, as if I were a god, to acquit him for their sake of any misconduct in office. 'If you have a weakness for tender young meat, have pity on the lad.' Then, in case I have other tastes, he begs me to listen to his daughter's whimperings. So then we tone down our anger a bit for his benefit. Isn't ours a splendid job—to be able to spit in the faces of the rich?

Bdelykleon. I'll make a note of that—spitting in the faces of the rich. But tell me what real advantages you get from this power over Greece that you claim to have.

Philokleon. Well, we have the right to inspect boys' private parts when they come to be registered.[39] And if Oiagros appears as a defendant, he doesn't get off until he has picked out the finest speech from the *Niobe* and given us a performance. And if a flautist wins a case, he rewards us jurors as we leave the Court by putting on his equipment and playing a recessional . . . And we aren't accountable for anything we do: that's an immunity which no other office holder enjoys.

Bdelykleon. Yes, that is impressive; on that one point I do congratulate you.

Philokleon. What's more, when the Council and Assembly can't decide how to handle some serious affair, they vote to hand over the offenders to the jurors.

And even that champion loud-mouth Kleon leaves us alone when he's looking for someone to get his teeth into. In fact, he takes us under his wing and shoos away the flies . . .

(*Philokleon goes on congratulating himself, until his son shows him that the jurors are not as privileged as he thinks. 'It is this passage which makes clear that the real object of Aristophanes' attack in this play is not the jurors themselves . . .'* *)

Bdelykleon. Now, listen to me, dad . . . First of all, do a few rough calculations—no need for a counting-machine, use your fingers. Take the sum total of all the tribute that comes in to us from our subjects, then add on to that the taxes, the various one-per-cents, the court-fees, and what we get from mines, harbours, markets, rents, sales of confiscated goods. That comes to two thousand talents, pretty near. Take from this a year's pay for six thousand jurors: one hundred and fifty talents, by my reckoning.[40]

Philokleon. You mean that not as much as a tenth of the revenues goes towards our pay?

Bdelykleon. You bet it doesn't.

Philokleon. And what happens to the rest of the money?

Bdelykleon. It goes to the men who swear: 'I shall not betray the rabble of Athens; I shall always fight for the masses.'[41] And it's you, father, who choose them as your masters; you get taken in by their fine phrases . . . You're no better off than a slave, while all of them, and their toadies, are in office, drawing salaries. If someone gives you your three obols, you're content—obols which you yourself sweated to get us, fighting in the navy and in the infantry and at sieges. Then on top of that you run about at their beck and call—and this is what gets my goat—when that mere kid, that pouf, the son of Chaireas, comes into Court, standing with his legs apart, like this, mincing and waggling his arse, and tells you to arrive punctually at crack of dawn to take your seat in Court. 'If any of you arrives after the bell goes, he won't get his three obols.' But *he* gets his advocate's fee—a drachma—even if he does arrive late.

A scene from another of Aristophanes' plays, *Wealth*, written in his old age, over thirty years after *Wasps*, shows how the reliance of the Athenians on

* D. M. MacDowell, *Aristophanes: Wasps* (1971), 218.

prosecution by volunteers, an integral feature of participatory democracy, provided scope for busybodies. (This had been introduced by Solon, who favoured a participating society, with members feeling responsible for one another, although he did not desire political, social or economic equality; see chapter III.) 'Sykophantes' was the term applied to a man who abused the system, or was alleged by wealthy defaulters to have abused it, whether out of excessive zeal or for private profit. The activity could be profitable because in certain types of case a successful prosecutor was rewarded with a substantial share of the fine exacted or the property confiscated; there was also scope for blackmail, and for hiring one's services to individuals who wanted their enemies to be prosecuted. On the other hand, being a *sykophantes* was, as Aristotle (p. 7) indicates, an offence for which a man could be prosecuted, though it is not clear how the offence was legally defined.

Aristophanes, *Wealth* 899–925

Sykophantes. I call on Zeus and the gods to witness the intolerable outrages these men are inflicting on me. I won't stand for it. To think that a good citizen and a patriot like me should be so ill treated!
Just Man. You a good citizen and a patriot?
S. There's none to equal me.
J. Well then, answer me a few questions.
S. Such as what?
J. Are you a farmer?
S. Do I look so thick headed?
J. A merchant, then?
S. Yes. Or at least I pretend to be, when convenient.
J. But what are you really? Have you learnt any trade?
S. Not bloody likely.
J. How do you live, then, and what on, if you don't do anything?
S. I am a supervisor of public affairs; private affairs, too: everything.
J. You? Who put you on to that game?
S. I do it because I like it.
J. And you call yourself a good citizen, you who break into people's homes and get yourself loathed for meddling with things that are none of your business.
S. So serving my country to the best of my ability is none of my business, you nitwit?

J. Then serving one's country means playing the busybody?
S. Giving one's support to the established laws and stepping in to prevent the commission of offences: that's service to one's country.
J. But hasn't the state put jurors on the job precisely for that purpose?
S. But who is to bring the charges?
J. Anyone who likes.
S. Well, it's I who like. So the government of the country falls to me.
J. A bloody rotten protector the country's got, then. Wouldn't you like to live in peace, with nothing to do?
S. That's a sheep's life you're talking about. One must have something to keep one amused.
J. But won't you learn a new trade?
S. Not if you gave me the god of wealth himself, and all of Battos' silphion.[42]

DUTIES OF THE RICH

The chief victims of *sykophantai* were of course the rich, who could be accused, justly or unjustly, of failure to fulfil their obligations to the community. There was no regular direct taxation; but from 427, if not earlier, there were occasional direct capital levies in time of war, and there was a temptation to understate one's wealth. Evasion of such charges as customs duty, which was one of the main regular sources of state revenue, could also occur.

But above all the richest citizens were required to perform, in turn, certain costly services, known as liturgies. The principal services were those of acting as captain of a warship through a campaigning season and of acting as impresario for one or other of various musical, dramatic and gymnastic performances at religious festivals. Here again evasion was possible, but the evidence suggests that most rich citizens, and rich immigrants, took pride in performing them more expensively than necessary. An example is provided by the rich man, charged, it seems, with accepting bribes while in office and with embezzlement of public funds, who delivered in his own defence the speech, written for him by Lysias, from which the following passage is drawn. Lysias himself came of a wealthy family but was not a citizen; his father, a friend of Perikles, had as an immigrant established a shield manufactory in the Peiraieus, but the Thirty seized all the family's property and Lysias took up speech-writing to make a living after the restoration of democracy.

Lysias 21.1–5, 10–19

So much for the charges against me, gentlemen of the jury: you have had a sufficient explanation.

I ask you now to listen to the rest of what I have to say, so that you will be aware of the sort of man I am before you give your verdict.

I passed my enrolment test in the archonship of Theopompos (411–10); I was then appointed a producer for tragedy and spent thirty minas. Two months later I won first prize at the Thargelia with a men's dithyrambic chorus, having spent two thousand drachmas. In the archonship of Glaukippos (410–9) I spent eight thousand drachmas on pyrrhic dancers at the Great Panathenaia. Under the same Archon I won first prize with a men's dithyrambic chorus at the Dionysia, and I spent, including the dedication of the tripod,[43] five thousand drachmas; and in the archonship of Diokles (409–8) three hundred drachmas on a cyclic chorus.

Meanwhile I was serving as captain of a warship; I served for seven years and spent six talents. [44] And although I was incurring such heavy expenditure and was risking my life day after day on your behalf and was away from Athens, nevertheless I twice contributed to capital levies, on one occasion thirty minas, on the other four thousand drachmas.

Directly after I had sailed back to Athens—that was in the archonship of Alexias (405–4)—I served as producer of a gymnastic display at the Prometheia and won first prize, having spent twelve minas. Afterwards I was appointed a producer for a boys' chorus and spent more than fifteen minas. Next, in the archonship of Eukleides (403–2), I was a producer for comedy, for a play by Kephisodoros; I won first prize, and I spent sixteen minas, including the dedication of the equipment. Then at the Little Panathenaia I was a producer for boy pyrrhic dancers and spent seven minas.

I have won first prize in a warship race to Sunion, at a cost of fifteen minas; to say nothing of leading delegations to festivals and paying for the Arrhephoria and other such items, which together have cost me more than thirty minas.

That is the tally of my services to the community. If I had chosen to perform only those that were required of me by law, I would not have spent a quarter as much ... While I was captain of a warship, my vessel was the best equipped in the whole fleet ... You can imagine how much I had to spend on a warship so carefully fitted out, how much damage it did the enemy and what services it rendered to the community ...

But in spite of having faced so many perils on your behalf and having rendered my country so many services, I am not now asking for a reward for these services, such as others have received from you. No, I am merely asking not to be deprived of what I own; for I believe that it would be disgraceful if one who has given willingly were to be forced to give against his will. It is not that I care so much about losing my property; what I will not put up with is being humiliated, and getting no gratitude for what I have spent on you, while I see those who have dodged their obligations to the community being regarded as sensible because they have sacrificed none of their wealth on your behalf.

So, if you are convinced by my arguments, you will not only return a just verdict, you will also be serving your own interests. For you are aware, gentlemen, of how scanty the state's revenues are, and you are aware that, scanty as they are, those in charge are battening on them. You should therefore regard the wealth of those willing to perform public services as the state's surest source of income. So, if you are wise, you will take as much care of our property as of your own private property, for you will bear in mind that all our property will be at your service, as in the past; and I imagine that all of you must realize that I shall be a much more efficient custodian of my own property than those who act for you as custodians of state property. If on the other hand you make me a pauper, you will be doing yourselves an injustice as well as me, for others will share out my property among themselves, as they have in other cases.

You should also bear in mind that it would be much more appropriate for you to be giving me some of your property than to be making claims against me on mine; and you ought to be sorry for me if I were to become a pauper, instead of envying my wealth. You should pray to the gods for other citizens like me, who, instead of coveting your property, spend their own for your benefit. I do believe, gentlemen of the jury—please don't take offence, but I do believe that there would be much greater justice in your being registered by the Inspectors as having property of mine in your possession than in my facing this serious charge of being in possession of public funds.

For what has been my conduct as a citizen? I am economical in my personal expenditure; I take pleasure in performing public services. I pride myself, not on the wealth that remains in my possession, but on what I have spent for your benefit; for I take the view that I am personally responsible for what I have spent, whereas what I own was left to me by others; and I am confident that, whereas my enemies bring malicious and unjust charges against me because of what I own, I can look to you for just protection because of what I have spent...

No one could say that I have benefited at your expense by holding numerous offices, or that suits damaging to my reputation have been brought against me, or that I have been responsible for anything disreputable, or that I have rejoiced in my country's misfortunes: I believe, and I believe you know, that my conduct as a citizen, both in public and in private, has included nothing for which I need to apologize. So I ask you, gentlemen, to maintain the same opinion of me as in the past, and not only to recall my public services but to bear in mind also my personal conduct; for I hold that the most exacting of services to the community lies in living at all times a decent and sober life, never falling into the grip of self-indulgence, never carried away by greed for material gain, and in so conducting oneself that one gives none of one's fellow citizens any ground for complaint or any encouragement to take one to Court.

WAS ATHENS UNIQUE?

What Aristotle (384–322) says in his *Politics* shows that the main features of Athenian democracy existed in other Greek democracies, so far as their resources allowed, whether in imitation or as the outcome of parallel development; for it was not Aristotle's way to generalize from a single instance.

Aristotle, *Politics* 6.2

The basis of a democratic political system is liberty. (People constantly make this statement, implying that it is only under democracy that men experience liberty; every democracy, they assert, has liberty for its aim.) One criterion of liberty is ruling and being ruled in turn. For the democratic idea of justice is that there should be arithmetical equality, not equality based on merit.[45] (But when this idea of what is right prevails, the masses are bound to be in control, and whatever the majority decides is final and is right. For, they say, every citizen must have equal power. The result is that in democracies those without means have more control over things than those with means, for they are more numerous, and majority decisions prevail.) That, then, is one criterion of liberty, one which all who are on the side of the people regard as a defining characteristic of this political system.

Another criterion is that a man may live as he chooses. For this, people say, is the rôle of a free man, just as it is the rôle of a slave to live in a way that he does not choose. This is the second defining characteristic of democracy. From it follows the idea that no one should be ruled by anyone, but that, failing this, people should rule and be ruled in turn. So we come back to the association of liberty and equality.

From these premises, and from this idea about rule, the following features of a people's régime are derived: that all should be eligible for every office; that all should govern each and each govern all in turn; that all offices, or at least all that do not require experience and skill, should be filled by lot; that there should be no property qualification for office, or at most an extremely low one; that few, if any, offices, apart from military offices, should be held twice, or more than a few times at most; that tenure of all offices, or at least of as many as possible, should be brief; that either the whole citizen body should act as a court of justice or else those who constitute the courts should be drawn from the whole citizen body, and that such courts should have jurisdiction, if not over everything, at least over most matters, including the most important, those of most consequence, for instance, investigations of the conduct of officials, questions of citizenship, and private contracts; that the Assembly should have ultimate authority over everything; and that officials should have ultimate authority over nothing, or over as few matters as possible ... that fees should be paid, if possible, to all those who attend the Assembly, sit in the courts of justice, and hold office, but failing that, to jurors, officials, councillors and those who attend plenary meetings of the Assembly, or at least to those officials who are required to mess together ... Such are the features that are shared by all democracies.

In Greece, where free and unfree men lived side by side, it was clear that what liberty meant, what characterized a free man, was not having to take orders. But in a political community orders have to be given and obeyed: so some members of the community will be in the position of slaves, unless all enjoy the right to some share, at least, in giving orders—unless, that is to say, there is at least some element of democracy. But if the demand for a share for all grows, as it did, into a demand for an equal share for all, *isonomia*, and if equality means, as most people took it to mean, what Aristotle calls arithmetical equality, 'the masses are bound to be in control'; *isonomia* turns out to mean *demokratia*, in the sense of control by the commons. We shall see that one of the main concerns of Aristotle, and those who thought like him, was with finding out how to avoid or to mitigate this evil.

One way in which it could be mitigated was by making it difficult for the masses to participate to any great extent. From what Aristotle says here, it is not clear whether many *poleis* did pay fees for service on juries or on the council or for attendance at meetings of the assembly; but what he says here and elsewhere clearly implies that some did. However, Rhodes is the only *polis* that he names in this connection, and there is very little evidence from other sources. It is generally thought that remuneration for any of these services must in fact have been a rare phenomenon. Partly for this reason, there may have been few, if any, other *poleis* in which participation was both as extensive and as intensive as it was at Athens, particularly in the latter half of the fifth century, when a citizen could often feel that what he was doing would have an effect far beyond Athens. Elsewhere much more may have been left, as a rule, to champions of the people, *prostatai tou demou*; although there are indications that, as one might expect, poorer citizens would turn up *en masse* at sessions of the assembly at which matters that closely affected them were to be discussed and voted on.

II. Origins of Greek Democracy: from Thersites to Tyrtaios

KINGS AND NOBLES AS RULERS

The events and adventures narrated in the *Iliad* and the *Odyssey* are presented by the poet as having happened long before his time: and so they had. Chieftains, that is to say, with the same names probably did perform not wholly dissimilar exploits in the thirteenth century; but both epics were composed not far from 700, soon after the Greeks had relearnt from the Phoenicians the art of writing, which they had forgotten for centuries; this meant that an oral epic that had been developing gradually could and would be stabilized, and perhaps considerably elaborated. Some scholars, however, think that the social setting in which the poems place the adventures is mainly that of the tenth century, others that it is mainly that of the eighth century—the result of elaboration of the epic at that time, qualified by memories, enshrined in it, of how things had been a few centuries earlier and by the attempts of bards to imagine how things must have been when everything in the life of chieftains was, as they believed, on a grander scale, morally and materially, than in their own day.

For us, looking for the roots of democracy, what is important is that in these poems we find ourselves in small communities in which commoners, whether farming on Ithaka or serving with the expedition against Troy, are felt, at least in some passages, to be part of the community, with no yawning gulf fixed between them and the chieftains, the princes, despite the chieftains' alleged descent from the gods; and although every man's concern is concentrated for most of the time on himself and on his own household, his *oikos*, and, if he is noble, on his peers, participation by the commoners collectively—community action—is not out of the question. Nor is it unheard of for commoners to assert themselves, although they may fail to assert themselves when their betters would like to have them do so for their betters' benefit, and although an individual commoner may get into trouble for asserting himself for his own benefit against the wishes of his betters.

What is also important to note is that, in Homer's opinion, the Cyclops and his brethren were distinguished from Greeks not so much by being one-eyed as, first, by not being farmers, and, secondly, by having no rules of communal life and no machinery for community debate and community action.

Homer, *Odyssey* 2.1–81, 224–239 (extracts)

As soon as rose-fingered dawn had lit the east, Odysseus' own dear son . . . ordered the shrill-voiced heralds to call the long-haired Achaians to the place of assembly. The heralds gave the call, and they assembled swiftly. When they had assembled and all of them were gathered together, he rose to go to the place of assembly . . . All the folk gazed at him as he approached. He went to sit in his father's seat, and the elders made way for him.

The first to address the gathering was the hero Aigyptios . . . 'Listen now, men of Ithaka, to what I have to say. We have never met in assembly and there has been no sitting since the day when godlike Odysseus went forth with his hollow ships. Who has now assembled us thus? Which of our young men or of their seniors has felt so strong a need? Has he heard some news of an approaching army, of which he would give us a clear report, having been the first to learn of it? Or will he disclose in his speech something else that concerns the people? He is a good man, I do believe; he is lucky. May Zeus bring to prosperous fulfilment whatever his heart is desiring!'

Such were his words, and Odysseus' own dear son was grateful for what he had said. He remained seated no longer, for he was anxious to address the meeting. He stood up in the midst of the assembly, and the herald Peisenor, a man of shrewd counsel, placed the speaker's staff in his hands. First he fastened on the old man (*Aigyptios*) and spoke to him: 'Sir, the man of whom you speak is not far away, as you yourself shall soon learn—I am the man who has assembled the folk. It is mostly sorrow that has impelled me. I have heard no news of an approaching army of which I could give you a clear report, having been the first to learn of it. Nor can I disclose in my speech anything else that concerns the people: only my own need, the misfortune that has befallen my house. A twofold misfortune: I have lost my good father, who once was king among you here, and a gentle father; but now there is something even graver, something that will soon tear my whole house asunder and destroy my entire livelihood. My dear mother is beset, against her will, by suitors . . . They keep coming to our house day after day, slaughtering oxen and sheep and fat goats for their feasts and drinking our glowing wine quite recklessly: our substance is being wasted . . .'

Thus he spoke in his anger, and threw the staff to the ground, bursting into tears: and pity swept over all the folk . . . Then Mentor rose to speak. He had been a companion of blameless Odysseus, who on departing with his ships had entrusted to him his whole household, bidding him heed his aged father and keep everything safe and sound. It was he who now addressed them with words of good will . . . 'Listen now, men of Ithaka, to what I have to say . . . There is no thought for godlike Odysseus among any of the folk over whom he ruled, to whom he was like a gentle father . . . I am angry now with the people, that you all sit in silence and do not raise your voices against the suitors, they being few and you many . . .'

Odyssey 9. 106–115

'We came to the land of the Cyclopes, an unruly people, who have no settled customs. So great is their trust in the immortal gods that they do not stir a finger to plant or to plough; no, all things grow unsown and untilled, wheat and barley and vines, whose grapes give wine in plenty; Zeus sends rain to swell the yield. They have no assemblies in which they take counsel and no settled customs; no, they live high up on lofty mountains in deep caves, each man fixes customs for his children and his wives, and they do not care about one another.'

Iliad 2. 179–181, 207–282

(*Athena instructs Odysseus*) 'Go now among the Achaian folk, do not hold back, stiffen each man's spirit with your proud words, do not let them drag their smooth ships down to the sea . . .'

So he made his way through the army, giving orders; and they hastened to the place of assembly, back from the ships and the tents, noisily, as when a wave of the glistening sea roars across a long beach and the tall water crashes.

Then they all sat down and stayed quietly in their places. Only

Thersites, uncontrolled of speech, kept wrangling: his mind was richly stored with jarring phrases, for use in vain, discordant strife with princes. But to the Argives his behaviour seemed ridiculous; he was the meanest scoundrel that came to Troy, bandy-legged, lame in one foot, with humped shoulders pressing down on his chest, while his sparsely-thatched head was like a pot skewed in the firing. Achilles detested him, and so did Odysseus, for he was always needling them; and now he was pouring out a stream of shrill insults at godlike Agamemnon. This angered the Achaians intensely; their hearts were full of indignation. But he went on shouting reproaches at Agamemnon: 'Son of Atreus, what cause have you for complaint? What more do you want? Your tents and your ships are full of bronze, there are many women in your tents, carefully selected, for we Achaians give you the first choice when we storm a fortress. Or do you covet gold, which some son of the horse-taming Trojans might get you from Ilion as ransom, someone whom I or another of the Achaians might capture and bring back? Or a young woman to make love to, whom you could keep apart for yourself? It is unbecoming for you, our leader, to bring troubles on the sons of the Achaians. O you weaklings, you who disgrace the Achaian name, women, no longer men, let us make our way home with the ships and leave this fellow here to gloat over his privileges, until he finds out whether or not it is on us that he depends. This is the man who has lately insulted Achilles, a far finer mortal than he, for he took his prize and has kept it for himself. But Achilles, it seems, feels no anger in his heart; he lets the matter slide: else, son of Atreus, this would have been your last offence.'

Such were Thersites' reproaches to Agamemnon, shepherd of the people. But godlike Odysseus quickly went and stood by him and looking at him grimly spoke hard words: 'Thersites, you talk at random, piercing orator though you are. Hold your tongue and do not try to match yourself against princes, for let me tell you that there is no more worthless creature than you among all who have come with Atreus' sons to the siege of Ilion. So kindly do not hold forth to princes in that familiar fashion, pouring insults on them, with an eye to getting home. We cannot yet tell for certain how this venture will turn out, whether we sons of the Achaians will have a good homecoming or a bad one. Today it is Atreus' son, Agamemnon, whom you persist in insulting because the Danaan heroes offer him many gifts; you hold forth jeeringly. But I will tell you something that shall surely come to pass. If I catch you making a fool of yourself like this again, then may Odysseus' head no longer rest on his shoulders, may I no longer be called Telemachos' father, if I do not take you and strip off your precious garments, your cloak and tunic and whatever covers your private parts, and send you sobbing from the assembly to the swift ships, disgraced by a sound thrashing.'

Thus he spoke, and struck him with his sceptre on back and shoulders; and he cowered and burst into tears, and a bloody weal rose up on his back where the golden sceptre had struck. Then he sat down and was silent, and sadly, with a helpless look, he wiped away his tears. The others laughed, sick at heart though they were, and thus would a man speak to his neighbour as he looked on: 'Ha! Of all the thousands of splendid things that Odysseus has done, giving a lead with his advice and marshalling the fighting, this is by far his best deed yet among the Argives, stopping the speech of that rash slanderer. Never again will his proud spirit impel him to anger princes with insulting words.'

Thus spoke the masses. Then Odysseus, stormer of citadels, stood up, holding his sceptre, and beside him owl-eyed Athena, in the shape of a herald, bade the folk be silent. So the greatest and least of the sons of the Achaians together listened to his words and considered his advice . . .

This passage shows what those who in the following centuries stood up for freedom of speech and for the sharing of political rights had to build on, and what attitudes, of arrogance and of awe, they had to stand up against.

We may, however, feel that Homer was here accommodating himself to wishful thinking on the part of his lordly patrons, to whom a Thersites or a Hesiod was perhaps already quite a familiar figure, and perhaps not so easily suppressed as Thersites here, especially when there was no threat from outside to make commoners thankful for the prowess of their leaders.

THE NOBLES CHALLENGED

Be that as it may, in the world that Homer presents to us one of the settled customs is that those of noble birth should be in charge and commoners should give them their support, for what that support may be worth. This meant also that those who fought on behalf of the community were in charge, for this was an age in which the decisive fighting was between noble champions: that was the convention.

In such a society, as life became more settled, the king could easily sink to the level of his peers. So monarchy gave way to what Aristotle sometimes calls aristocracy, rule by the most able, sometimes oligarchy, rule by a wealthy minority.

It was in a Boiotian community dominated by nobles that the poet Hesiod lived, round about 700, and although the nobles probably left commoners to their own devices for the most part, it appears from what he tells us that they did insist that disputes should be brought to them for settlement. This was, in a way, a step forward from self-help; but Hesiod's experience of their handling of a dispute between himself and his brother Perses led him to include a bitter indictment of their greed and unrighteousness in a long poem which he wrote, giving moral and practical advice to his fellow peasants.

Hesiod, *Works and Days* 202–285

And now I will tell a fable to our lords, who know its meaning. Thus spoke the hawk to the nightingale with speckled throat, as he bore her aloft among the clouds, gripped fast in his claws, and she, pierced by his crooked claws, was weeping pitifully; masterful were his words: 'Dear lady, why shriek? One far stronger than you now holds you fast, and you must go wherever I take you, singer though you are. And I will make a meal of you, if I please, or let you go. He is a fool who tries to set himself against the stronger, for he cannot win, and he gets hurt as well as humiliated.' So said the swiftly flying hawk, the long-winged bird.

But you, Perses, heed right (*diké*) and keep clear of presumption (*hubris*), for presumption is bad for men of low estate. Even for a man of quality presumptuous acts are risky; he founders beneath them when he falls into delusion. The better road to take is on the other side, the side of right, for right comes out ahead of presumption in the end: but only by suffering does the fool learn ... A rushing sound is heard when those who devour gifts drag Right where they will, those who twist rights in passing judgment; and Right then wraps herself in mist and goes about the *polis* and the homes of the people, weeping and bringing mischief to men who have driven her out and have not given her a straight run.

Origins of Greek Democracy: From Thersites to Tyrtaios

But those who give strangers and those who belong to the community their rights without bias and do not step aside from what is right find their *polis* flourishing and their folk basking in prosperity... For those, however, who indulge in presumption and cruel conduct the son of Kronos, far-seeing Zeus, has fixed the right reward: often a whole *polis* suffers for a bad man who transgresses, scheming presumptuously...

Give your attention, lords, to the right of which I speak, for the deathless gods are near at hand amongst men and take note of all who twist rights to oppress their fellows, caring naught for the wrath of the gods; for there are thrice ten thousand deathless messengers of Zeus going about the fruitful earth, keeping watch over mortal men; they keep watch on rights and on cruel deeds as they roam, wrapped in mist, over all the world. And then there is the maiden Right herself, child of Zeus, honoured and reverenced among the gods who dwell on Olympos; whenever anyone hurts her by his twisting, treating her with contempt, she straightway sits by her father, Zeus son of Kronos, and tells him of men's unrighteous schemes; and in the end the People pay for the wickedness of their lords, who in their baneful scheming bend and twist men's rights when they give judgment. Beware of this, lords, make your pronouncements straight, although you swallow gifts, put any twisting of rights from your thoughts...

The eye of Zeus, seeing all and understanding all, beholds what is now happening here, if so he will, and fails not to mark the sort of right that the *polis* keeps within it. May neither I myself now be righteous among men, nor my son—for it will be bad to be righteous—if the party who is in the wrong is to obtain the greater right. But no, I do not believe that all-wise Zeus will let things end like that. And you, Perses, lay up in your heart what I am saying; hearken to right and give up all thought of force. For the way (*nomos*) ordained by Zeus for man is this: fish and beasts and birds of the air are bound to prey on one another, not knowing what is right; Right is his most precious gift to man. For he who knows the rights of things and is ready to say what he knows is rewarded with prosperity by far-seeing Zeus; but he who deliberately tells lies and forswears himself to bear false witness, damaging right in his irremediable infatuation, condemns his posterity to decay...

In these lines we see the beginnings of moral and political philosophy, the dawn of awareness that within the limits of the *nomos* ordained for man by Zeus there is a difference between how things are, as a result of the lords' twisting of *diké*, and how they might and should be: so one need not say, 'Whatever is, is right'. There is also a sense of the interdependence of those who constitute the community, the *polis*: the People, the *demos*. But Hesiod is still content to try to make his lords, and himself, believe that Zeus will defend the right: although he believes that the whole People suffers for their lords' misdeeds, he does not suggest that commoners should be given a share in running things.

POWER TO THE HOPLITES

In a passage in his *Politics* Aristotle summarizes the political changes that began to occur in Greek communities soon after Hesiod wrote, as he saw them in retrospect.

Aristotle, *Politics* 4.13

The first political system that came into being among the Greeks after kings ceased to rule was an association of the fighting men: those who owned horses in the first place, because strength and superiority in war lay with those who owned horses; for a body of heavy infantry is useless without organization, and people at that time had no experience in such matters, and orderly dispositions were unknown. That is why strength lay with those who owned horses. But as states became more populous and the infantrymen gained strength, the number of those with a share in the political system increased. That is why what we would now call 'polities' were formerly called democracies. The earliest political systems, however, were naturally oligarchic when they were not monarchic; for owing to the smallness of the populations there was not much of a middle element, and being both small and ill organized it put up with being ruled.

What Aristotle says here should not be taken as giving us an insight into the development of Greek communities and Greek warfare in the seventh and sixth centuries which we could not otherwise obtain, for he probably had little more in the way of relevant contemporary evidence than we possess, and less material evidence. However, he puts his finger on a change that most historians believe to have been significant.

Before the seventh century only the few who owned horses seem to have counted much in war, as Aristotle says and as Homer indicates, hard though this may be to explain rationally, since they did not normally fight as cavalry. But during the century there was a gradual spread of new fashions in armour, weapons and mode of combat. The new fighting man who emerged from this development came to be called the hoplite; the formation in which he fought, the phalanx. The new mode of combat was less individualistic and called less for prowess than for collective solidarity and weight of numbers. So more men were drawn in, men not of noble birth, but who could afford the requisite armour and weapons, but not a horse: mostly peasants, it seems.

At first, in spite of their new importance, they 'put up with being ruled'; but gradually they gained 'a share in the political system'. Although socially 'a middle element', they might now think of themselves as constituting the People, the Demos; and so the resulting systems might be called democracies, although there is in fact no evidence that this term was ever applied to a system in which the numerous poorer members of the community were excluded from power, or indeed that the word was used at all before the fifth century.

There is no evidence to support (or to refute) Aristotle's assertion that in his time such systems (which certainly did then still exist) were called simply 'polities'. Elsewhere in the *Politics*, and in other writers, we find 'polity' used to denote any constitutional régime, or else any political system whatsoever.

THE SPARTAN EXPERIMENT

There is reason to suspect that the Spartans achieved the first such 'hoplite polity'; for by the seventh century that small community, who called themselves Spartiates, numbering not more than ten thousand warriors, had achieved a precarious ascendancy over the inhabitants of a number of surrounding communities—the *Perioikoi*, 'dwellers around about', as they came to be called—and also over a large mass of serfs, the Helots; and in the process they had seized enough land, which the Helots farmed for them, to give each adult male Spartiate sufficient means to serve as a hoplite, and to be free of the need to do any productive work.

But such a set-up, which was exceptional in the Greek world, created an acute need for military efficiency and solidarity, to prevent disruption of the set-up, whether by hostile outsiders or from within. A Spartan poet of the seventh century, Tyrtaios, composed poems to foster the requisite spirit among the hoplites.

Tyrtaios 9

> I would not think a man worth mentioning
>   For nimble-footedness or wrestling skill,
> Or if he had a Cyklops' build and strength
>   Or could outpace the Thracian Boreas,
> Or if he matched Tithonos in good looks
>   Or Midas and Kinyras in his wealth
> Or outshone Pelops in his kingliness
>   And had Adrastos' gift of honeyed speech
> And every virtue, save a warrior's might.
>   A man, you see, is of no use in war
> Unless he can stand firm in face of death
>   And lay about him grimly in close fight.
> That is true worth; that gains the finest prize,
>   The best reward that men, while young, can win.
> The *polis* and the people all are helped
>   When every man stands firmly in the ranks
> Without a thought of timorous retreat,
>   Putting his life at risk courageously,
> Urging his fellows on with cheering words.
>   A man like this is valuable in war;
> The close-knit phalanx of the enemy
>   Is scattered as he stems the battle's tide.
> He meets his death in the forefront of the fight,
>   A glory to his town and folk and kin,
> When many well-aimed shafts have pierced his shield
>   And, bursting through his breastplate, have struck home.
> Then young and old alike lament his death
>   And all the people mourn their grievous loss.
> His tomb is greatly honoured by all men;
>   So are his sons, and sons' sons, evermore.
> A man's renown and glory never fade,
>   He still lives on, though laid beneath the ground,
> If he stood firm and fought courageously
>   For land and kin, till Ares struck him down.
> But if he escapes the grip of levelling death
>   And gains the victory for which he prayed,

Then young and old alike will honour him,
    He'll know much joy in his declining years,
Admired by fellow citizens as he grows old.
    He'll never meet with hurt or disrespect;
Both young and elderly, at his approach,
    Will rise up from their seats or step aside.
This is the peak of excellence a man should strive
    To reach, by giving all his heart to war.

But exhortations could not be enough. In a system in which so much depended on all those who could fight, they naturally would not for long 'put up with being ruled'. Moreover, it seems that (as in other communities) some Spartiates had acquired much more land than others; and when the Messenians, who had been made Helots in the eighth century, rose against their masters in the seventh, there was an opportunity for rank-and-file Spartiates to press both economic and political demands.

Aristotle, *Politics* 5.7

In states in which control is in the hands of a few ... conflict is likely to arise ... when some are excessively poor while others are excessively wealthy. This happens particularly in time of war. It happened at Sparta at the time of the Messenian War. This is clear from the poem of Tyrtaios entitled *Eunomia*—men who were ground down by the war demanded that the land should be redistributed.

We do not have the lines of Tyrtaios to which Aristotle refers, and we do not know for certain whether rank-and-file Spartiates were given more land at this time. What we do know is that they were given sovereignty, of a sort. The main features of a new political order were submitted to the priestess of Apollo at Delphi, and, having received Apollo's approval, they were regarded as constituting an oracle. As such, and as an ordinance for the community—a *rhetra*—they were preserved and observed at Sparta through succeeding centuries. Tyrtaios echoed and commented on them in one of his poems, in which he describes the visit of the kings of Sparta to Delphi (for reasons which had been forgotten, Sparta had two royal houses, reigning simultaneously; and in the new order there continued to be two kings, while in most other Greek states kings lost their thrones).

Tyrtaios 3

> Lord of the silver bow, Apollo golden-haired,
>   Powerful from afar, spoke thus from his rich shrine:
> 'The kings, whose rank stems from on high, shall first
>   Advise, for lovely Sparta is their care,
> They and the Elders; then the common folk
>   Shall utter their response in straight decrees,
> Speaking fair words and acting righteously,
>   But shall not twist the advice they give the state.
> The will of the mass of the people shall prevail.'
>   Such was the message Phoibos sent to us.
> They heard what Phoibos said, and brought back home
>   Words to be turned into deeds, a god's commands.

From this and from other evidence it appears that thenceforward proposals prepared by the Council of Elders together with the Kings had to be submitted to the Assembly of Spartiates, who could accept or reject but not 'twist', that is to say amend, them. The assembled Spartiates also chose annually the five chief officials, the Ephors.

Thucydides shows us the Assembly at work two centuries later, in 432.

Thucydides 1.88

Sthenilaidas, in his capacity as Ephor, put the question to the Lakedaimonian Assembly.[1] Then, declaring that he could not discern which shout was louder, for they vote by shouting, not by ballot, he said: 'Those of you, Lakedaimonians, who consider that the treaty has been broken and the Athenians are in the wrong, rise and stand over there,' showing them a place; 'those who are not of that opinion, on the other side.' They rose and stood in two groups: and those who considered that the treaty had been broken were much more numerous. The authorities then summoned the allies and told them that they had decided that the Athenians were in the wrong.

That, then, is what was achieved by the first Greek thrust towards democracy.

Aristotle, as we saw just now, mentions that the title *Eunomia* was given (not necessarily by Tyrtaios) to a poem by him which was evidently concerned with this thrust. The word *eunomia* (which was used already by Hesiod, who sets Eunomia alongside Diké, Right, as a superhuman figure) means a state of things in which *nomos*, a society's whole fabric of customs and rules, is working *eu*, satisfactorily. From this time onwards *eunomia* occurs repeatedly in discussions about the political and social order. It comes to be seen as a state of affairs which, without making any revolutionary changes, men can bring into existence for themselves.

But by the time of Aristotle Sparta's *eunomia* had been dislocated.

Aristotle, *Politics* 2.9

Some say that the best political system is a blend of all systems. For that reason they approve of the Spartan system: they say that it combines oligarchy and monarchy and democracy, the Kingship representing monarchy, the Council of Elders oligarchy, and the office of Ephor democracy, since the Ephors are chosen from among the people. Others, however, say that the Ephorate is dictatorial, and that the element of democracy is found in the communal meals and the rest of everyday life. . . .

One thing on which there is agreement is that if a state is to have a good political system men must be freed from menial tasks: but how they are to be given this freedom is not easy to see. For example, in Thessaly there are serfs, the *Penestai*; but these have often attacked the Thessalians. Likewise the Helots have often attacked the Lakonians (*meaning the Spartiates*): they are always on the lookout for any misfortune that may befall them . . . Even if nothing goes wrong, it is troublesome to have to be constantly concerned with how to deal with a serf element. If they are kept on a loose rein, they get above themselves and claim equal rights with their masters. It is clear that the Lakonians, who have this problem with Helots, have not yet found a satisfactory solution . . .

One might go on from this to criticize the inequality of property ownership; for the situation at the present day is that some Spartans own an excessive amount, others extremely little, because the land has fallen into the hands of a minority. Here again the legal provisions are unsatisfactory. The legislator [2] laid down that buying or selling of existing estates was to be censured, which was a sound rule; but he made it permissible for anyone to give land away or bequeath it, which was bound to lead to the same result. Almost two-fifths of all the land now belongs to women, partly because heiresses are numerous,[3] partly as a result of the giving of large dowries . . . Consequently, whereas there is enough land to support fifteen hundred cavalry and thirty thousand heavy infantry, there are fewer now than one thousand. History has shown the badness of these arrangements: a single military defeat proved too much for Sparta.[4] Shortage of men has been her undoing . . .

The arrangements concerned with the office of Ephor are also unsatisfactory. This office has independent control over the most important of public business; but the Ephors are chosen from among all the people, with the result that the office often falls to men who are not at all well off, and their poverty makes them venal . . . Again, because their power is so great, indeed virtually dictatorial, even the Kings have been forced to truckle to them, and this too has damaged the political system; aristocracy has turned into democracy.

However, this office does hold the system together, for the people keep quiet, since they have a share in tenure of the highest office; and whether this was the legislator's intention or has come about accidentally, it suits the situation. For if a political system is to survive, all sections of the citizen body must be in favour of it and want it to remain in being. That is the attitude of the Kings, because of the honour that is paid them; of the gentry, because of the Council of Elders, membership being the prize awarded to those best qualified; [5] and of the people, because of the Ephorate, for all are eligible.

On the other hand, although it is right that all should be eligible, they should not be chosen in the way in which they are chosen now, which is childish . . .[6]

The arrangements for communal meals, the so-called *phiditia*, were also not worked out satisfactorily by whoever originally instituted them.[7] The messes should be run at public expense, as in Crete. In Lakonia every man has to contribute individually, and as some of them are not at all well off and cannot meet the expense, the effect is the opposite of what the legislator intended. For these communal meals are meant to be a democratic institution, but the way in which they are organized is far from democratic. For men who are by no means well off it is not easy to participate, but this is the traditional way of determining citizenship: the man who cannot pay his due is excluded . . .

The whole social order is aimed at developing one kind of excellence, military prowess, this being useful for the winning of power. Consequently, after surviving a long series of wars, they have come to grief since achieving hegemony,[8] since they do not understand how to live at peace, and have never gone in for any of the kinds of training that are more important than training for war.

As Aristotle indicates, the Spartiates had imposed on themselves an elaborate framework of social institutions, designed to promote discipline and an illusion of equality; but by the fourth century, as he explains, inequalities of wealth between the so-called Equals had become so great that some of the Equals had lost their status. Early in the century, Kinadon, one of these Inferiors, tried to organize a revolution, bringing in Helots and *Perioikoi*, in addition to others like himself, and *Neodamodeis*, Helots whom the Spartiates had freed in return for military service but had then left, it would seem, in a social limbo.

Xenophon, *History of Greece* 3.3

A conspiracy was reported to the Ephors, and Kinadon was named as its organizer: a sturdy and energetic young man, but not one of the Equals. When the Ephors asked the informer how Kinadon had said that the plan would be carried out, he replied that Kinadon had taken him to the edge of the Agora and asked him to count how many Spartiates there were in the Agora. 'And I,' he said, 'after counting a King, and Ephors, and Elders, and about forty others, asked, "Why, Kinadon, did you tell me to count these men?" He replied: "You must consider them as your enemies; but all the other people in the Agora you may regard as allies—more than four thousand."' He said that when they met people on the roads, Kinadon described one or two now and again as enemies but all the rest as allies; and when they came across people on the farms that belonged to Spartiates, he described one, the master, as an enemy but the many others on each farm as allies.

When the Ephors asked the informer how many, according to Kinadon, were in the conspiracy, he said that Kinadon had told him that only a few reliable people were in contact with the leaders, but that these few said that they were in contact with all the Helots, *Neodamodeis*, Inferiors and *Perioikoi*. Whenever conversation in these sections of society turned to the Spartiates, they said, no one could conceal that he would gladly eat them raw.

When they went on to ask him where the conspirators expected to get weapons from, he said that Kinadon had told him that the inner circle did have sufficient weapons, and as to the masses, he took him into a smithy and showed him large stocks of knives, swords, skewers, axes, choppers and reaping hooks. Kinadon said that all the tools with which people work the land and timber and stone would serve as weapons, and that most other craftsmen had plenty of implements that they could use as weapons, especially as their opponents would be unarmed.

Finally they asked him at what time the rising was to begin. He said that he had been instructed to stay in town. When the Ephors heard this they judged that it was a well-organized plot and were extremely alarmed. They did not even summon the so-called Little Assembly, but approached the Elders individually...

After Kinadon had been arrested and questioned, and had made a full confession, naming his associates, they ended by asking him what his object had been. He replied: 'I wished to be inferior to no one in Lakedaimon.' After that, they bound him, neck and arms, in a collar and dragged him and his associates round the town, scourging and goading them as they went. So they got their punishment.

III. Democracy and Society: Athens and Syracuse

Although we find signs of the self-assertiveness of ordinary men in Greek communities, and of their will to work together, from the earliest times of which we have knowledge—as passages quoted in the previous chapter show—the movement towards participatory democracy would not have gone as far or spread as widely as it did had it not been for the example set by the Athenians. And the Athenians would not have gone as far, but for two accidents.

The first of these was the existence of a supply of silver-bearing ore within Athenian territory. This supply, exploited energetically from the second half of the sixth century onwards, was as important, relatively, as a supply of coal or oil has been for some modern states. For one thing, if the Athenians had not discovered a rich vein of ore at a crucial moment, they would not have decided to strengthen their navy to such an extent as to make it a major social factor. Moreover, without the advantage of a continuing supply of silver, they might not have gone as far in their experiment with so costly a mode of politics; and without it they might not have persisted in their experiment after they had lost the flow of tribute from subject states which naval power secured for them for seventy years or so during the fifth century—this had largely paid for an ambitious foreign policy, so that for a time most internal revenues could be used for domestic purposes.

The second was the emergence and rise to leadership of six extraordinary men, in an almost unbroken sequence extending over a century and three-quarters: Solon, Peisistratos, Kleisthenes, Themistokles, Perikles, Kleon. We have already encountered the last three; we shall shortly meet the others.

Of these six, only Kleon was not of the landowning nobility; he had inherited a prosperous tannery, and to that he owed the leisure for politics which the others owed mainly to ownership of land (leisure, not luxury: the wealth of the Athenian upper class was very modest compared with the wealth of the aristocracy and the bourgeoisie in many other societies, earlier and since). Therein lies Kleon's greatest importance. For one thing, it must have made ordinary Athenians, who had thitherto submitted to a mystique of leadership bound up with birth, feel, 'If Kleon, why not me?' Moreover, whereas an ambitious young member of an old landowning family, with friends among his peers, could look to an inherited following to start him, at least, on a political career, Kleon had to look to 'the people' at large; and even if he encouraged them to rely on him as their champion, he was also necessarily encouraging their self-importance, for he needed their active support. For these reasons he had a uniformly bad press, unlike any of the others: the two contemporary voices that speak loudest to us are those of men who detested him—Thucydides, a nobleman, whose own political career, moreover, was blighted by Kleon, or so he may have felt; and Aristophanes, an admirer of the old ways.

Kleon, then, was a man of the people, and made the most of that rôle. Why should the other five have undermined the ascendancy of the established élite into which they had been born by promoting changes that would give the people greater power?

Each, it is safe to say, aspired to win admiration and fame: but in that they were not alone among their peers; they differed from them only, it may be said, in being more boldly imaginative in the means that they adopted—and more successful in making their mark. But although none of them had any obvious precedent to inspire him, since each went a little further, it may be that each had somehow come to believe strongly in the moral rightness of what he set out to do, and it may be that each had a more idealistic view of the capacity of the people than most of his contemporaries. A few would attribute idealism even to Peisistratos the dictator; a few would deny it even to Solon, who foreswore personal power. Assessments of the other three are more evenly divided: Plato, for one, would have us take at least as low a view of Themistokles and Perikles as Thucydides and Aristophanes would have us take of Kleon.

Greek writers did not go at all fully into the rôle of leadership; discussion was concentrated, as we have seen and as we shall see below, on the respective merits of rule by the masses or by an élite, and on the qualifications that all of those involved needed to possess.

DEBT AND DISCONTENT

Aristotle's account of the development of the political system at Athens, which precedes the description of its working in his time that was quoted in part in chapter I, is the only connected account that we possess of the growth of a democracy in Greece. It is far from satisfactory, because the evidence at Aristotle's disposal was scanty, especially for the earlier stages, and of uneven quality. However, he made good use of the testimony of

Democracy and Society: Athens and Syracuse

Solon, which gave him and gives us direct insight into the state of Athens in the early years of the sixth century. Unfortunately most of the preceding part of Aristotle's account is lost; our only manuscript, on a damaged papyrus roll, opens in the middle of a narrative of events that occurred about 632. It continues as follows:

Aristotle, *Constitution of Athens*

2. Afterwards there was conflict for a long time between the notables and the masses; for the way in which the community was organized was wholly oligarchic. In particular, the poor were the serfs of the rich, they and their wives and children. They were called 'sixth-parters', for that was the portion of their produce that they had to render. All the land was under the control of a minority, and if the poor failed to render their portion, they and their children were liable to seizure; everyone contracted loans on personal security until the time of Solon, who was the first man to stand up for the people.

For the masses, then, the hardest and most painful feature of the system was their serfdom, but that is not to say that they did not have other grievances, for they had, practically speaking, no share in anything . . .

3. The qualifications for holding office were birth and wealth . . .

(*There follows information about the chief officials of those days, the Nine Archons, who held office for one year only, exemplifying already what became the will of every* polis *to limit the power of individuals.*)

The Council of the Areopagites had the function of seeing that the laws were observed, but in fact it performed most of the important work of government; it had full authority to control and punish all who stepped out of line. The Archons were chosen, as I have said, on a basis of birth and wealth, and it was they who became Areopagites . . .

5. This being the state of affairs, with the poor slaving for the rich, the people set themselves against the notables, and for a long time there was intense conflict between them; but eventually they appointed Solon as Archon to effect a settlement, placing the whole system in his hands, after he had composed the elegy that begins

> I see Ionia's most ancient land
> Torn asunder, and there is deep grief in my heart.

In this poem he defends each of the two parties against the other and states the case for each, and he then goes on to urge them both to give up their effort to come out on top.

In birth and reputation Solon was one of the highest in the land, but in wealth and in his mode of life he stood between the extremes. There are, it is agreed, various clear indications of this, and in particular his own poetry provides evidence, when he advises the wealthy not to try to get more than their due:

> Calm the violent passions in your hearts;
> You have had more than your fill of many good things.
> Put limits on your grand ideas; we shall not
> Submit, nor will all things be as you wish.

And he always puts the whole blame for civil conflict on the rich. That is why he says in the opening lines of his elegy that he fears 'greed and pride', presenting these as the causes of the conflict ...

(*There follows a description and discussion of some of Solon's measures as Archon, beginning with the first, cancellation of all debts and prohibition of personal security for loans. It seems that these must have brought about a liberation of all the serfs, the sixth-parters, who had previously, according to Aristotle, constituted a very large section of the population (and thus the freeing of the soil, of which Solon boasts below); for subsequently we never hear of serfs (as distinct from slaves, who were imported in gradually increasing numbers), but we do hear of numerous free peasants. Aristotle's assessment of what Solon did for the commons politically is given in a passage from his* Politics *quoted below, p. 61.*)

FAIR SHARES AND EQUAL RIGHTS

Constitution of Athens, continued

11. So Solon opposed both sides, and although he could have made himself a dictator by allying himself with one side or the other, he preferred to rescue his country from ruin and give it the best possible system of laws, getting himself disliked by both parties for his pains.

12. All agree that this was his way, and he himself in his poetry refers to his achievements in the following words:

> I gave the people such prerogatives as they need,
>   Neither lowering their status nor enhancing it.
> Those who had power, of whose wealth men stood in awe,
>   I took pains to protect from anything unseemly.
> I stood and held my strong shield over both;
>   I would not let either prevail in despite of justice.

Again, in expressing his views on the masses and how they should be treated, he says:

> This is how the people will best follow their leaders—
>   If they are not too slackly reined and yet are not compelled.
> Satiety breeds insolence, when great prosperity
>   Comes to men whose minds are not well trained.

And again, in another place, he speaks of those who wanted to split up the land:

> They came for plunder, nourishing fat hopes,
> Each of them thinking he would win great wealth
> And I reveal a harsh mind behind my coaxing words.
> Idle were their expectations; now they are angry with me
> And all look at me askance, as at an enemy.
> Wrongly: for what I promised I accomplished, with God's help,
> And other things I did were not in vain. Nor do I wish
> To use despotic force to do things, nor to see
> Good men and base with equal shares of our land's rich soil.

(Redistribution of the land remained, along with cancellation of debts, the economic aim of popular movements throughout Greek history, land remaining the most cherished form of wealth and the most important source of livelihood, and indebtedness an endemic ill. In other communities, those who fought for equal political rights for all citizens sometimes also proclaimed, and sometimes achieved, these other aims (as did some who intended or achieved dictatorship). At Athens we do not hear again of either demand for five centuries; but some modern writers believe, although there is no direct evidence for this, that Peisistratos, the dictator mentioned below, divided among poor Athenians some of the estates of noble landowners who went into exile after he came to power.)

Again, on the subject of the cancellation of debts, and those who had been in bondage before and were freed by the 'shaking off of burdens', he (*Solon*) says:

> My plans induced the people to unite;
> I did not pause until they were fulfilled.
> Best witness to this, before the bar of time,
> Is Mother Earth, greatest of Olympian gods,
> From whose black flesh I took the many signs
> Of servitude: and thus I made her free.
> I brought back many to our god-given land
> Who had been sold abroad, some wrongfully,
> Some by due process; others, too, in flight
> From pressing debts, whose tongues had quite unlearnt
> Their Attic speech, so long their wanderings.
> Some here at home were shamingly enslaved,
> Trembling before their masters' whim: them too
> I freed. Combining right with might,
> I went the whole way to make good my promises.
> The laws I published were of equal force
> For high and low: I laid down one straight line
> For all. Suppose some evil, grasping man
> Had held the power that I held: he would not
> Have kept the people in check. For had I wished
> To please the people's enemies, or do
> Instead the things *their* enemies had planned,
> I would have robbed our state of many men.
> And so I was attacked from every side,
> Standing at bay, a wolf beset by hounds.

And again, hitting back at those on both sides who criticized him afterwards, he says:

> To the people I say this, if I must utter a plain rebuke:
>   What now is theirs would have been beyond their dreams.
> Those of higher estate, superior in strength,
>   Should thank me and consider me their friend.

If anyone else, he says, had held the position that he held,

> He would not have kept the people in check; he would have churned
>   Things up, to get himself the butter from the milk.

Democracy and Society: Athens and Syracuse

> But I stood in the space between the contenders
> Like a boundary mark.

Solon described as *Eunomia* the state of affairs that he had sought to establish, and that the Athenians must by their own efforts maintain. He relied largely on a change of heart. In his day this did not occur, but in the long run his teaching, embodied also in his measures, did have a deep effect on Athenian thought and behaviour under democracy.

In the *Politics* Aristotle considers differing assessments of Solon's work and of its relation to later changes.

Aristotle, *Politics* 2.12

Some consider that Solon was a good legislator, for he put an end to an oligarchy that was quite undiluted, freed the people from slavery, and instituted Athens' 'traditional democracy.'[1] This was a well-balanced political system: the Council of the Areopagus was oligarchic, the filling of offices by election was aristocratic, the law courts were democratic.[2] It seems likely that the Council and the filling of offices by election were in existence before his time, and were simply retained, but that he brought the people into the picture by making everyone eligible to serve as a juror.

It is for this that some people criticize him: he made the other elements ineffective by giving control over everything to the law courts, the jurors for which were chosen by lot; for when the Courts became powerful, this led to a dictatorship of the people: everyone courted the people's favour, and that is how present-day democracy came into being. The Council of the Areopagus was crippled by Ephialtes and Perikles,[3] Perikles instituted a fee for jurors, and the various popular leaders kept going further along this path until they had created present-day democracy.

However, this does not seem to have been Solon's intention; it came about rather as a result of circumstances. For instance, the pre-eminence of Athenian seapower in the Persian Wars was due to the people, and this gave them a great opinion of themselves:[4] they then chose leaders of poor quality, men of the better sort being in opposition. Solon seems to have given the people only as much power as they were bound to get, the right to elect officials and to call them to account.[5] If the people did not have even that much power, they would be slaves, and enemies of the established order. On the other hand, he arranged for all the officials to be chosen from among the notables and the men of means; those in the lowest property class, the *thetes*, were not eligible for any office.

In the middle of the sixth century a nobleman named Peisistratos succeeded, after two false starts, in installing himself as dictator, with the help of hired professional soldiers and after exploiting the grievances of several sections of the population—thus defying the *nomos*, the established practice, of the *polis*. He was, however, by all accounts a benevolent despot, who made Athens more prosperous, by enforcing social peace and giving help to the peasants, and more prominent in the Greek world. Probably one of the effects of his rule was to give some ordinary Athenians greater self-confidence and a stronger awareness of being Athenian, weakening their ties to local grandees and to local religious cults which the grandees dominated.

His son Hippias, who succeeded him on his death in 527, seems to have been a somewhat less skilful and less lucky ruler, and in 511 another ambitious nobleman, Kleisthenes—who had held high office under Hippias, but had later gone into exile—managed to oust him with the help of a Spartan army.

Aristotle, *Constitution of Athens*

20. After the overthrow of the dictatorship, there was a struggle between Isagoras son of Teisandros, a friend of the dictators, and Kleisthenes, of the Alkmaionid family. In the conflict between their followings Kleisthenes came off the worse; he then won the people over to his side by offering to place the system under the control of the masses ...
21. Having made himself champion of the masses, he effected the following changes, three years after the overthrow of the dictatorship, during the archonship of Isagoras (508–7). First, he distributed all the citizens among ten new constituencies, in place of the four that then existed; he wanted to mix them up, in the hope that more would participate in the running of things ... Then he created a Council of Five Hundred, in place of the Council of Four Hundred (*which, according to Aristotle, Solon had instituted*), fifty, instead of one hundred, from each constituency ... He also divided up the state's territory into thirty sections: ten sections were composed of the demes

around the town of Athens, ten of the demes along the coast and ten of the demes in the interior. These sections he called *trittyes*. He assigned three sections, by lot, to each constituency, so that each constituency would include a part of all three regions ... (22) As a result of these changes, the political system became much more favourable to the people than Solon's system had been ...

Aristotle says elsewhere (*Politics* 3.9) that this creation of new constituencies also enabled Kleisthenes to include in them 'many aliens and slaves'. Part of what lies behind this assertion, which he must have drawn from someone who disliked Kleisthenes' work, was that Solon, in addition to liberating enslaved Athenians, had offered citizenship to immigrants skilled in some craft; and Peisistratos may have been equally liberal. Conservative nobles would not have liked such persons, who might well not be subservient, and indeed Aristotle tells us (*Constitution of Athens* 13) that after Hippias was ousted and they were for a time dominant again 'there was a revision of the citizen rolls, on the ground that many who did not belong were participating in citizen rights'.

Kleisthenes, or one of his supporters, chose or coined the slogan *Isonomia*, which echoed *Eunomia*, to advocate the changes that he introduced. It was probably not intended to imply opposition to the ideal of *eunomia*, or to the continued exercise of leadership by able members of the nobility (such as Kleisthenes himself); but it introduced and emphasized the idea of equality of rights.

NAVAL POWER AND THE RULE OF THE MASSES

Constitution of Athens, continued

22. ... During the archonship of Nikodemos (483–482), after the discovery of a vein of silver-bearing ore at Maroneia, the state acquired a surplus of one hundred talents from the working of the mines. Some recommended that the silver should be distributed among the People, but Themistokles prevented this ... Instead, he got a hundred warships built. It was with these warships that they fought at Salamis against the foreign invaders.

Thucydides also has something to say about the ideas and achievements of Themistokles, whose foresight he greatly admired.

Thucydides 1

93. It was Themistokles who persuaded the Athenians to finish the fortification of the Peiraieus, which had been begun earlier, in a year in which he had held office. He was influenced both by the attractiveness of the site, which has three natural harbours, and by the advantageous position for winning power that the Athenians would occupy if they became a naval people. It was he who first ventured to tell them that they should lay a firm hold on the sea; and he was, in effect, now helping to lay the foundations of their empire . . .

With these tall thick walls he intended to keep off enemy attacks; he thought that they might be adequately defended by a small body of those least fit for active service, so that the rest would be free to serve in the fleet. It was particularly on the fleet that his thoughts were concentrated . . . He thought the Peiraieus more valuable than the town of Athens, which lay inland. Indeed, the advice that he constantly gave to the Athenians was that if ever they were hard pressed on land they should go down to the Peiraieus and defy the world with their fleet.

(*After Themistokles' time, in about 460, a compromise scheme was adopted, linking Athens and its harbours.*)

107. The Athenians began to build two long walls from the town down to the sea, one to Phaleron and one to the Peiraieus.

This meant that the navy, manned largely by the poorer Athenians, especially those living in Athens and the Peiraieus, would become unquestionably more important than the army, composed largely of landowners, great and small; and in the event of the invasion of Athenian territory by an enemy land force the Athenian countryside might be abandoned, the population withdrawing inside the long walls. So we are not surprised to hear from Thucydides that when the Spartans and their allies had occasion to send an army into Central Greece in 457:

There were persons in Athens secretly negotiating with them, in the hope of putting an end to democracy and to the building of the Long Walls.

One reason why the Athenians took to attaching so much importance to naval power, and why, moreover, they could contemplate temporary abandonment of their farming land, was mentioned at the beginning of chapter I: their reliance on imported grain. The beginnings of this dependence reached back to the early years of the fifth century, if not further. Normally they could and did pay for this largely by growing olives, for which much of the land was better suited, there being a market for olive oil overseas, particularly in some of the regions in which grain could be grown advantageously.

Plato, in one of his last works, *Laws* (in which he has ceased to use Socrates as his mouthpiece) emphasized the consequences of reliance on naval power, as they appeared to him.

Plato, *Laws* 4.707

The Athenian visitor: If a state depends on naval power, that means that in the hour of salvation honours are conferred on a section of the armed forces that is of inferior quality. What is more, if those responsible for victory are helmsmen and petty officers and ordinary seamen, a motley assortment of individuals of no real quality, how can there be any correct distribution of honours? But, failing this, how can a state be correctly run?

Kleinias the Cretan: It would be almost impossible. But all the same, my friend, the naval battle at Salamis (*480*) against the Persians was what saved Greece. Or at least that is what we Cretans believe.

The Athenian visitor: Well, yes, that is what most Greeks say, and foreigners too. But we—that is to say, I and my friend Megillos here—maintain that the land battle at Marathon (*490*) was the beginning of the salvation of Greece, and that the victory of Plataiai (*479*) was what finally settled the issue. Moreover, we maintain that these victories raised the moral stature of the Greeks, and that those other victories lowered it—I say 'those', for alongside the battle of Salamis one must place the battle of Artemision (*480*).

An illuminating little essay has come down to us, mistakenly included in manuscripts among the works of Xenophon: its author is writing to explain to friends somewhere else in Greece that, morally distasteful though Athenian democracy is, it nevertheless has its own logic. This essay was probably written in the early years of the Peloponnesian War, the war between the Athenians and the Spartans and their allies which broke out in 431 and continued, with intermissions, until 404. We may, for convenience, adopt the English convention of referring to the author as 'the Old Oligarch'. He is the earliest witness to what democracy had turned out to mean, from the point of view of the élite: not only have ignorant, low-grade people been admitted to power, they are ruling *in their own interest*.

[Xenophon], *Constitution of Athens*

1. My opinion of the Athenian political system is this. I do not at all approve of their having chosen a system of this kind, because by making this choice they have chosen to make things better for men who are good for nothing than for men of worth. That is the reason for my disapproval; but what I propose to demonstrate is that, having made this decision, they go the right way about protecting their system and about managing affairs which other Greeks think that they mismanage.

In the first place I would point out that if at Athens the poor and the commoners are given advantages over the gentry and the men of means, this is as it should be, for the simple reason that the commoners provide the motive power for the navy and give the state its strength. For the helmsmen and the masters at arms and the corporals and the look-out men and the shipwrights are the men who give the state its strength, far more so than the infantrymen and the gentry and the men of worth. This being the case, it seems right that the offices of state, both those that are now filled by lot and those to which election is by show of hands, should be open to all, and that any citizen who wishes to speak in the Assembly should be allowed to do so.

Moreover, the commoners do not call for a share in those offices that ensure the state's safety when they are in worthy hands and bring it into danger then they are not; they do not think that a share in the Generalships or the cavalry commands should be assigned to them. That is because they recognize that they derive greater benefit from not holding these offices themselves and from allowing the most influential men to hold them instead. They are, however, eager to hold all those offices which involve the receipt of a fee and the chance of making private profit.

Another thing that surprises some people is that in every sphere of life greater consideration is shown to poor, good-for-nothing commoners than to men of worth. However, it can be shown that it is precisely in this way that democracy is protected. For if poor men and commoners and riff-raff prosper and multiply, they will broaden the base of democracy; but if the rich and the men of worth prosper, the commoners are strengthening their own enemies. All the world over, the best people stand opposed to democracy, for among the best people you will find the greatest respect for discipline and right conduct and the strictest regard for values, whereas in the ranks of the people at large you will encounter ignorance, indiscipline and immorality at every turn; their poverty, lack of education and ignorance —the result, in some cases, of lack of money—make them more prone to disgraceful behaviour.

Some people might say that it was a mistake to allow everyone to speak in the Assembly and serve in turn on the Council, and that these rights should have been given only to the ablest and best. But here too the Athenians show sound judgment in allowing worthless persons to speak. For if men of worth spoke, and served on the Council, this would be beneficial for those like them, but quite the opposite for common folk. As things are now, anyone who likes, any worthless individual, may get up and speak; and he comes up with something beneficial to himself and to those like him.

Someone may ask, 'How can such a person recognize what is good for himself or for the people?' The Athenians realize that his ignorance and immorality and good will profit them more than the ill will of a man of worth, however capable and clever.

Granted that a state with such ways of doing things will not attain a high moral standard; nevertheless, they are the most conducive to the maintenance of democracy. For the commoners do not want to have a properly ordered system under which they will have the status of slaves; they want to be free and to govern. They do not care much about the neglect of law and order. What you regard as a lack of *eunomia* has in the eyes of the common folk the merit that it gives them freedom and power; whereas, if you want *eunomia*, that would mean having the ablest men legislating in their own interest; it would mean having a government composed of men of worth, who would impose discipline on the ne'er-do-wells and put a stop to maniacs having seats on the Council or enjoying free speech or indeed attending the Assembly. And of course the result of such reforms would be that commoners would indeed be reduced to the status of slaves.

People object also that at Athens slaves and immigrants lead thoroughly undisciplined lives: striking them is forbidden, and a slave will not stand out of the way for you. I will explain the reason for this peculiar state of affairs. If it were legal for a free man to strike a slave or an immigrant or a freedman, an Athenian would often be mistaken for a slave and receive a beating, for at Athens commoners are no better clad and no better looking than slaves and immigrants.

What may cause further surprise is that the Athenians allow their slaves to live in luxury; some of them, indeed, live in great style. But in this, too, it would appear that they are sensible. For in a state that possesses naval power, it is essential to have slaves working for pay, so that we can take a proportion of their earnings, letting them run free; and where there are rich slaves, it ceases to be advantageous that my slave should be afraid of you. In Sparta my slave would be afraid of you, but in Athens, if your slave is afraid of me, there is a danger that he will hand over his earnings to save his skin.

That is why we have extended freedom of speech to slaves in their dealings with free men: and the reason why we have extended it to foreigners in their dealings with citizens is that the state needs immigrants, to sustain the multitude of crafts, and the fleet: that is probably why we have granted freedom of speech to foreigners also . . .[6]

When it is a matter of providing choral or dramatic or gymnastic performances, or operating a warship, the accepted arrangement is that the rich pay the expenses, and the people are thus provided with entertainments and with warships. Whether they are singing or running or dancing or serving in the fleet, the people expect to receive money, so that they may be the gainers, while the rich grow poorer. (So also in the law courts: the people care less about justice than about their own advantage). . . .

2. . . . As to sacrifices and festivals and temples and sanctuaries, the people are aware that the poor cannot individually provide sacrifices and feasts and equip themselves with temples and build a great and beautiful city, but they have found a means of achieving all this. The state sacrifices quantities of victims at public expense; the people enjoy the festivities and share out the victims.

As to gymnasiums and baths and dressing rooms: some of the rich have these for their own private use, but the people have built numerous public wrestling schools and dressing rooms and bathing establishments, and the rabble get more benefit from these than the fortunate few . . .

So I forgive the people their democracy, for no one can be blamed for looking after himself. However, if any one who is not by birth a commoner deliberately chooses to live in a democratic rather than an oligarchic state, he can only have vicious intentions;[7] he must have come to the conclusion that a wicked man can escape detection more easily in a democratic state than in an oligarchy . . .

3. I know that some people complain against the Athenians because at times a man is unable to transact a piece of business with the Council or the Assembly even if he sits waiting a whole year. This does indeed happen at Athens, simply because the volume of business to be handled is such that they are unable to give audience to all and send them off. How in the world could they, . . . when they have to decide more private and public suits and scrutinize the conduct of more officials than all the rest of mankind put together, and when the Council has to have frequent debates on the war, on ways and means, on legislation, and on the matters constantly arising at home and in relation to Athens' allies, and receive payments of tribute from the allies, and superintend the dockyards and the temples? Is it at all surprising that with so many matters on their hands they are unable to settle everyone's business?

Some say that if you have money in your hands when you approach the Council or the Assembly, you will get your business dealt with. I would agree that one can often get things done at Athens if one pays to get them done, and even more would get done if even more people offered money. But I am also quite certain that the state is not capable of getting through everything that people want done, however much gold and silver one might offer.

Here are some of the matters on which a decision has to be reached: if someone fails to equip a warship, or builds on public land; what persons, each year, are to finance the dramatic and choral performances at the Dionysia, the Thargelia, the Panathenaia, the Prometheia, the Hephaistia; and four hundred persons have to be appointed every year to run warships, and every year claims for exemption have to be adjudicated. In addition, the eligibility of incoming officials has to be scrutinized, war-orphans have to be examined, prison warders appointed. These matters arise every year: from time to time the Council has to pass judgment on military cases and other cases of wrongdoing that crop up suddenly, such as some extraordinary outrage or sacrilege. I omit a whole series of other matters; I have mentioned the most important, except for the assessment of the tribute to be paid by Athens' allies: this generally occurs every four years ...

All this being so, I maintain that things at Athens could not be organized otherwise than they are now, give or take a little here or there. No great alteration could be made without subtracting some element of democracy. Many ways could be found of improving the political system, but it is not easy to find satisfactory ways of improving the system while maintaining democracy, except, as I have said, by slight additions or subtractions ...

Down to the time at which this essay was written, members of the élite, the *gnorimoi*, who were, unlike the writer, prepared to adapt themselves positively to a democratic political system, retained a disproportionate prominence in public life, as the writer points out in his fashion: 'the commoners do not think that a share in the Generalships should be assigned to them'. The most famous was Perikles.

One of the last, and most brilliant, of such men was Perikles' ward, Alkibiades, whose connections, wealth, eloquence and charisma made him extremely influential but whose arrogant defiance of conventions won him many enemies. In 415 he fled to Sparta rather than face a charge of sacrilege which, according to Thucydides (6.28), had been 'taken hold of by those who could least endure him because he stood in the way of their obtaining undisturbed leadership of the people, and who thought that if he were once removed, the first place would be theirs'—men of the style of Kleon (who himself had been killed in action seven years earlier). Such people asserted that his alleged sacrilege was 'part and parcel of a scheme to overthrow the democracy', pointing, for proof, to 'the general and undemocratic licence of his life and habits'.

Thucydides reports what Alkibiades said to the Spartans, who were regarded as opponents both of democracy and of dictatorship, in an impudent endeavour to ingratiate himself with them.

Thucydides 6.89

Some have judged me unfavourably because I have leant rather to the side of the people. 'The people' is a designation comprehending all who oppose arbitrary power, and my family have always been hostile to dictators; that is how we acquired the role, which we have maintained, of popular leadership. Besides, Athens being a democracy, it was necessary to adapt ourselves in most ways to prevailing conditions.

However, in an atmosphere of contempt for law and order, we endeavoured to follow a relatively moderate political line. There were some who, in recent times as in the past, tried to lead the mob into deplorable excesses: they are the men who got me thrown out; but we stood up for the community as a whole, and we believed that it was our duty to help to maintain the form of government under which Athens enjoyed the utmost greatness and freedom, the form of government that had been handed down to us. Democracy: we men of sense knew, of course, what to think of it, and I have perhaps as much cause as anyone to heap abuse, seeing how grievously I have been wronged; but there is nothing new to be said about a patent absurdity, and we did not think it safe to try to alter it while your enmity was bearing down on us.

THE PELOPONNESIAN WAR

In Aristotle's view, experiences in the Peloponnesian War strengthened the desire among ordinary Athenians to participate in the running of things, beyond the point which they had reached, according to the Old Oligarch, very early in the war, of being 'eager to hold all those offices which involve the receipt of a fee and the chance of making private profit'.

Aristotle, *Constitution of Athens* 27

Fees for service in the Courts had been introduced by Perikles ... Some complain that subsequently the Courts deteriorated, since ordinary men have become increasingly keen to put themselves forward for selection, more so than men of the better sort ...

Then, in the forty-ninth year after the battle of Salamis, the war with the Peloponnesians broke out. During this war the people of Athens were cooped up in the town, and they became accustomed to being paid from public funds while they were on campaigns. And so, partly of their own free will, partly under pressure of circumstances, they chose to take over the running of the political system.

After the surrender of the Athenians in 404, the democratic régime was replaced, as we have seen, by a junta of thirty backed by the victorious Spartans; but in 403 the Thirty were ousted as the result of a popular rising, in which the Spartans, after some hesitation, acquiesced. To quote Aristotle once again:

Constitution of Athens 41

After the people had regained control of things, they established the political system which exists at the present day. Since they had effected their return by their own efforts, they would appear to have had the right to take the political system into their own hands. Between then and now there has been a steady increase in the effective power of the masses, for the people have assumed control of the whole set-up, everything being directed by decrees of the Assembly and by decisions of the Courts of Justice, in which the people are the masters. Even the judicial functions of the Council have passed into the hands of the people, and this would appear to have been a sound change, for small bodies are more easily corrupted than large, whether by money or by favours.

To begin with, payment for attendance at the Assembly was not allowed; but, when people failed to attend although the Presiding Committee tried many devices to induce the masses to turn up to provide a quorum, first Agyrrhios introduced a fee of one obol, then Herakleides of Klazomenai, nicknamed The King, two obols, then again Agyrrhios a fee of three obols.

So although, as we have seen in chapter I, participatory democracy was working in many ways more successfully at Athens during the eighty years or so that followed the Peloponnesian War than at any time or place before or since, it was also, in a sense, on the wane. For defeat had cost the Athenians their empire, and the efforts that they made during the first half of the fourth century to recover at least some part of it proved more costly than remunerative. Consequently the community now had less to spend on social benefits and amenities and on remuneration for those performing civic functions; and some of what there was had to be spent, as Aristotle here explains, on tempting enough citizens to attend routine meetings of the Assembly to provide a quorum.

This was partly because people felt less free to neglect whatever means they had of making a living for themselves, partly because defeat and the loss of empire caused some falling off of enthusiasm. Merely to 'take turns at ruling and being ruled' was less exhilarating than to have the sense of controlling the destinies of the Greeks.

Democracy and Society: Athens and Syracuse

So the Athenian People were further now than they had been in Perikles' time from being the aristocracy of which he dreamt (see chapter IV, p. 87).

THE ECONOMICS OF DEMOCRACY

This is the context in which Xenophon published his pamphlet *Ways and Means*. One way of looking at it is as an attempt to realize Perikles' dream; but what Xenophon himself had in mind was rather to enable the Athenians to cultivate the qualities that the Spartans cultivated, or were supposed to cultivate. In his youth Xenophon had been a great admirer of Spartan society, to the point of fighting, at one moment, with the Spartans against the Athenians, thus condemning himself to long years of exile from Athens; but meanwhile closer acquaintance with Sparta had brought growing disillusion, and in his old age he became genuinely anxious to help the land of his birth, to which, it seems, he had returned.

His proposals have points of contact with those which Isokrates was putting forward at the same time, around 355 (see below, chapter IV, pp. 97 ff.). They could be called more utopian; they could also be called more practical.

Xenophon, *Ways and Means*

1. The character of communities depends on the character of their leaders: that is what I have always believed. However, some of the leading men of Athens have been claiming that they know as well as anyone what is right, but that the poverty of the masses compels them to treat our allies less justly than they would otherwise. That is why I have set out to look for ways in which our citizens could gain a living from their own property, as in justice they should; for I believe that if this could be achieved, it would alleviate both their poverty and the misgivings with which we are regarded by the Greeks . . . (*Xenophon begins by pointing out how well endowed naturally Athens and Attica are, for fishing, quarrying and mining, and as a venue for traders.*)

2. One way in which we could add to these natural advantages would be by taking more trouble over resident aliens. They constitute, in my opinion, one of the best sources of revenue; for they provide for their own upkeep, they do a great deal of good to the community in which

they reside, but they do not receive any support from the state; on the contrary, they pay a poll-tax ...

(*Xenophon therefore suggests that they should be exempted from conscription for infantry service, that the wealthier should be enrolled in the cavalry—which in Xenophon's eyes, at least, would constitute a great honour—and that those judged 'worthy' should be allowed to buy building-sites, although land-ownership was normally reserved for citizens. If such steps were taken, 'probably every stateless person would want to come and settle in Athens, and this would increase the revenues'.*

He goes on to describe the natural advantages of the Peiraieus as a trading centre, and to suggest how the state could increase its attractiveness at little or no cost. Turning to state projects that would require an outlay of capital, he suggests ways in which both rich Athenians and foreigners could be induced to subscribe the requisite capital, 'perhaps even other republics, and, I hope, some kings and dictators and satraps, if they were to be commemorated in perpetuity as Benefactors of the Athenian People'.

However, the project to which he pins his highest hopes is public purchase of thousands of slaves, whom the state, following the precedents already set by private slaveowners, would rent out to persons taking concessions in the state's silver mines; for he believes that both the supply of silver and the demand are virtually inexhaustible. If part of the revenues that would thus accrue to the state were to be ploughed back, purchase could continue 'until there were three slaves for every Athenian'. Although he does not say so, his remarks suggest that what was in his mind was that this would put Athenian citizens in a position resembling that of the citizens of Sparta, each of whom had several state-owned helots working his land for him.)

4. ... I have now explained how the community's affairs could be arranged to provide an adequate living out of public resources for every Athenian ... I venture to suggest that if my proposals were carried out the community would not only enjoy increased revenues; it would be better disciplined and more orderly and more capable of defending itself. For one thing, young men instructed to undergo physical training would take this much more seriously if they were supplied with rations in the gymnasia than do those who at present take part in torch races under the direction of gymnasiarchs. Again, those assigned to guard-duty in fortresses or to light-armed service

Democracy and Society: Athens and Syracuse

and frontier patrols would perform their tasks more efficiently if rations were provided in each case.

5. (*To ensure the smooth working of Xenophon's projects, the Athenians should turn to promoting peace throughout the Greek world, instead of fighting to gain ascendancy.*) If anyone supposes that, from a material point of view, war is more advantageous to the community than peace, I do not know a better way of deciding this question than by examining how things have worked out for the community in the past. You will find that in earlier days a great deal of money was accumulated by the state in peacetime, all of which was squandered in time of war; and that in recent times the effect of the war was that revenues of many kinds ceased, while the money that did come in was squandered in all sorts of ways, whereas since peace has been restored in the Aegean (*in 355*) revenues have increased, and the citizens are able to make use of them as they please.

Perhaps I shall be asked, 'What if someone wrongs us? Would you say that we ought to remain at peace even with him?' No, I would not say that. What I do say is that we could punish aggressors far more swiftly if we ourselves gave up wronging others; for the aggressors would find no allies.

Well, then, if none of my proposals is impossible, or even difficult, to put into practice; and if the result of putting them into practice would be that we should become more popular among the Greeks, and enjoy greater security and a higher reputation, and that the people would have plenty to live on, and the rich be relieved of military expenditure, while the state's wealth would enable us to celebrate festivals more splendidly than at present, to build temples, to repair fortifications and dockyards, and to maintain time-honoured payments to priests and Councillors and officeholders and cavalrymen—should we not put them into effect as soon as possible, so that we can see the community enjoying security and prosperity within our own lifetime?

If you are in favour of my proposals, I urge you to send to Dodona and Delphi to ask the Gods whether it would be meet and proper for the community to be organized in this way, both at the present time and for the future.

Although Xenophon lays stress on the desirability of making the Athenian People 'more popular among the Greeks' by forswearing predatory policies, one may be sure that he, like Isokrates, was interested also in ensuring that democracy did not become a tyranny of the poor over the rich. Hitherto this danger had been successfully avoided: political equality and social inequality had coexisted peacefully; partly because Athens as a community had remained relatively prosperous, despite the decline in public revenues; partly because rich and poor shared the pride, and the practical advantages, of being Athenians, over against those living in their midst whom they excluded; partly because the rich were regarded as useful, if not indispensable; and partly because at Athens, as in modern democracies, the rich could exercise influence in various ways to protect themselves.

But the danger always loomed; and at almost exactly the time at which Xenophon published his proposals for promoting prosperity and social harmony at Athens, something very different was being discussed in Sicily. We owe to Plutarch (c. A.D. 45–120) the story, which he tells in his *Life of Dion* (chapters 31–54), but for which we have unfortunately no contemporary evidence, of an attempt to re-establish democracy at Syracuse in 356, led by a man named Herakleides. After Dion, commanding a large army of mercenaries, had effected the overthrow of the dictator Dionysios II, Herakleides, who became commander of the Syracusan fleet, which was largely manned by poor citizens, put forward proposals for a new democracy, which involved 'a redistribution of the land and the houses, the argument being that equality is the source of freedom, while poverty reduces those who have no possessions to a state of slavery'. This is the only context in which a voice has reached us from the ancient world suggesting that democracy could not be a reality in a community in which there were gross inequalities of wealth. The assembled People voted in favour of this plan; but Dion, a friend and former pupil of Plato, who shared Plato's distaste for democracy and was a staunch defender of the landowning interest ('the notables and the gentlefolk', 'the knights', 'the best people'—Plutarch uses these customary designations interchangeably), was able to get it annulled shortly afterwards, despite the opposition of 'the mob of sailors and manual workers'; Herakleides was then assassinated, and Dion reasserted his personal rule.

IV. Attitudes to Democracy in Greece

THE FIRST REACTIONS

Pindar, *Pythian Odes* 2.81–89

Impossible it is for a crafty commoner to utter words that will prevail among men of quality. Yes, he fawns, I know, on one and all, forever wriggling his way amongst them. I have no part in his impudence. Let it be for me to show friendship to a friend; to my enemy always an enemy, I shall run him down like a wolf, moving this way and that as he twists and turns. In every order the straight-speaking man comes to the fore: under one-man rule, and when the clamorous throng is master, and when the wise protect the *polis*. We must not contend against God, who upholds one element for a time, then gives great might to another.

The ode by Pindar from which these lines come is the oldest surviving work to reflect the emergence of democratic government. He wrote it in his forties to commemorate the victory of one of his patrons, Hieron (dictator of Syracuse from 478 to 467), in a chariot race at some great festival; it is one of many elaborate encomiastic odes that he composed. Himself probably of noble birth, he was clearly happy in the world of the noblemen, preoccupied with their roles among their peers, and of the festivals, at once religious and athletic, about which he wrote; and that, rather than the writing of plays for a mass audience, being the vocation to which he had been drawn (having been born and reared in a community, Thebes, wholly dominated by a landowning nobility), he naturally praised the achievements of his patrons and of the communities to which they belonged. But although he had strong ideas about how men ought to behave, he did not directly express any political preferences: 'when he refers to the popular assembly of a democratic state as "the noisy host",

it is unsafe to assume that the description is meant to be pejorative'.*
However, pejorativeness does surely creep in.

It is anyhow interesting that a man who travelled widely in the Greek world had by this time come to accept that the dominance of a noisy Assembly was among the phenomena that he could expect to encounter, one of the manifestations of the inscrutable will of the gods, which they might destroy as abruptly as they had raised it up. The word *demokratia* may have been invented only very shortly before this ode was written, to describe political arrangements such as Kleisthenes had introduced at Athens and probably others elsewhere. The word had the force of a slogan, 'Power to the People', whether it was coined by the enemies of the new order—'that is what "equal rights for all" turns out to mean in practice'— or by its friends; and it may not be accidental that Pindar uses a word with the same component, *krat*, to assert that a commoner, clever flatterer though he be, cannot 'prevail', win power, among men of quality. But it is notable that he also holds that the straight speaker—most probably a nobleman who (as was traditional) had learnt how to speak persuasively and had the self-assurance to speak forthrightly—could likewise hold his own in an Assembly. At Athens such nobles were, as we have seen, still the leaders at this time; and this was probably the case in other states, too, in which the People had gained a large share of power.

A play by Aischylos (525–456), *The Suppliant Women*, is the oldest surviving work of literature to reflect the changes towards full democracy that had been made at Athens since the ending of dictatorship in 511. It may have been produced in 463, when further such changes, made in 462, must have been in the air.

Precisely what Aischylos thought about these changes is a matter of dispute. It may be significant that he introduced a seemingly favourable (and of course quite anachronistic) reference to the power of the assembled People into this play about the legendary daughters of Danaos—who, long before the Trojan War, are, with their father, seeking refuge in Argos from powerful suitors whom they detest, and are asking for protection in the name of Zeus, patron of suppliants—but on the other hand it is possible that Aischylos believed that what he represents as the decision of the People of Argos constituted a misguided defiance of the will of the gods.

---

* Hugh Lloyd-Jones, 'Modern Interpretations of Pindar', *Journal of Hellenic Studies* 93 (1973), 112.

Attitudes to Democracy in Greece 79

Aischylos, *The Suppliant Women*

King Pelasgos: Your plea concerns not merely my own house. 365
If the whole state of Argos is involved,
The populace must find the remedy.
I cannot promise anything, until
I have consulted all the citizens ...
The choice is hard, and not for me to make. 397
I say again: king though I am, I shall
Not act until the People's will is known ...
Chorus: We have already cause for gratitude 490
In having found such gentle sponsorship ...

. . . . .

Danaos: Daughter, good news: the Argives are with us; 600
The People's vote has granted us our plea.
Leader of Chorus: Father, you bring the gladdest of good news.
Now tell us how the question was resolved,
How many hands were raised, for and against.
Danaos: The Argives were unanimous: I felt
As though my aged heart were young again.
The air was stirred by right hands thrust aloft
As the whole People voted the decree.

. . . .

King Pelasgos: These words of ours are not inscribed on wood 946
Nor sealed up in a folded document;
They come to you clearly from free-speaking tongues.
So get you gone with all speed from our sight.

PROS AND CONS

In writing an account of the conflicts between Greek states and the kings of Persia and what caused them, Herodotos (*c.* 484–427) included much information about the earlier history, the society and the government of the peoples most deeply involved on both sides.

In his opinion, 'it was the Athenians who, after God, saved Greece';

but his attitude to Athens, and democracy, was as sensitively ambivalent as it was to much else that came within his experience.

After describing how they ousted a dictator in 511 and defeated a Spartan attempt in 508 to prevent the adoption of a basically democratic constitution and impose an oligarchy in its place, he continues:

Herodotos 5.78

The Athenians went from strength to strength, thus proving that equality is an excellent thing, not in one way only but in many. For while they were under a dictatorship, they were no better at fighting than any of their neighbours, but once they were rid of dictators they became by far the best. This shows that while they were held down they fought badly on purpose, like men that work for a master, but when they were set free each was eager to achieve something for himself.

Shortly afterwards he tells the story of Aristagoras—a prominent citizen of Miletos, one of the leading Greek states on the west coast of Asia Minor —who visited European Greece in 499, trying to get help for a revolt of the Greek states in Asia Minor against Persian rule.

Herodotos 5.97

After he had been turned out of Sparta by King Kleomenes, Aristagoras went on to Athens, for Athens was the next most powerful state. He came before the Assembly and used the same arguments as he had used at Sparta . . . Apparently it is easier to fool a multitude than an individual, for although Aristagoras had failed to impose on Kleomenes, speaking man to man, he was successful with thirty thousand Athenians. They were convinced by his arguments and voted to send twenty warships to help the Ionians . . .; and these ships were the beginning of trouble both for the Greeks and for the barbarians.[1]

In an earlier section of his work, in describing the rise of Persia, he reports a meeting of seven Persian nobles who had in 521 assassinated a Median priest, or Magus, who had usurped the Persian throne. Despite his insistence on the veracity of his report of what was said at this meeting, it is

Attitudes to Democracy in Greece

generally thought that Herodotos is in fact mirroring debates about the best mode of government such as were taking place among Greeks in his own time.

Herodotos 3.80–83

Speeches were made to which many of the Greeks give no credence; nevertheless, they were made.

Otanes recommended that the management of affairs should be placed in the hands of all the Persians. 'My view,' he said, 'is that we should no longer have a single ruler, for this is neither pleasant nor good. You know how far Kambyses went in his violence, and you have experienced the violence of the Magus. How can monarchy be fitted into the scheme of things, when it allows a man to do whatever he likes without being answerable? If the best of all mankind were to rise to this position, he would cease to think as he thought before. The advantages that a monarch enjoys foster pride, while envy inheres in human nature. A man with both these afflictions is wholly evil . . .

'But rule by the People has, firstly, the finest of names, *isonomia*[2] and, secondly, the People do none of the things that a monarch does: offices are filled by lot, the holder of an office is answerable for what he does, all questions are put up for general debate. I therefore propose that we do away with monarchy and raise the People to power, for in the multitude all things are comprehended.'

Such was the view of Otanes. Megabyxos, however, recommended the setting up of an oligarchy. These were his words: 'All that Otanes said in favour of abolishing despotism I would echo; but in calling on us to hand over control to the People he did not hit on the best of ideas. For there is nothing more unintelligent or more violent than a crowd; a crowd is good for nothing. To escape from a despot's violence only to be caught up in the violence of an unruly mob would be utterly intolerable. What a despot does, he does knowingly; the common folk do not even know what they are doing. How could they, since they are untaught and have had no experience of the finer things of life? They rush in and sweep forward unthinkingly like a river in flood. Let the enemies of the Persians rely on the commons; we will choose a group of the best men and give them the power, for we ourselves shall be among them, and it is natural that the best counsel should come from the best men.'

This was the opinion that Megabyxos put forward. Lastly, Darius expressed his view, as follows: 'What Megabyxos said about the People was, I think, well said ... Where commoners rule there cannot fail to be corruption; and when there is corruption in public life, firm friendships are formed, for those involved gain their ends by putting their heads together. And so it goes on, until some champion of the commons puts an end to their activities. As a result, he is reverenced by the commons; and in their reverence they make a monarch of him: which again proves that monarchy is best ...'

Euripides (c. 485–c. 406) went much further than Aischylos in conscious anachronism, putting contemporary ideas and debates into plays peopled by characters from the legendary past. Scion, probably, of a relatively wealthy family (as were, indeed, most Greek writers), he was thought to be no friend of democracy; but he knew how to make his characters state a case for or against it as he thought appropriate. His *Suppliant Women* are the mothers of seven noble warriors who had been killed in an Argive attack on Thebes, begging Theseus, king of Athens, for help in recovering their sons' bodies from Kreon, king of Thebes. The play was produced in about 422, after nearly ten years of war between Athenians and Peloponnesians (who had the Thebans as allies), seven years after the death of Perikles, and at the time of the ascendancy of Kleon. We catch echoes both of the gibes of Aristophanes and of the version which Thucydides gives us of Perikles' 'funeral speech'.

Euripides, *The Suppliant Women* 399–441

Herald: Who is the master here? To whom should I
Report the words of Kreon? ...
Theseus: Sir, first I must correct your opening words.
You seek a master here. We are not ruled
By any single man. This state is free.
The People govern, taking power in turn
In yearly groups. Nor do we give to wealth
A larger share; the poor man gets no less.
Herald: It's my move now. You've given me a piece,
So I'm one up. The state from which I come

Attitudes to Democracy in Greece

Has one man in control and not a mob.
No orator can sway us to and fro
With flattering speeches, for his private gain ...
The People can't see through persuasive words:
How can they, then, direct a state aright?
They act in haste: to learn what's best takes time.
But let's suppose a poor farm labourer
Could get some learning; even so, his work
Keeps him from seeing to affairs of state.
The better sort think times are out of joint
When one of low degree, a ne'er-do-well,
Can with his tongue win following and fame.
Theseus: Clever, this herald; a debater, too.
You challenge me to contest: listen, then.
A despot is the ruin of a state.
For, first, there are no common laws; one man
Holds sway alone, a law unto himself.
Equality's lost too. With written laws
Justice must be the same for rich and poor;
The weak, if in the right, can crush the great.
And freedom means as well: 'Who wants to speak?
Step forward, any man with good ideas.'
There's scope for the ambitious; those who aren't
Keep quiet. Here is true equality.

PHILOSOPHICAL SUPPORT

Among those who reflected during the fifth century on the modes of political life of the Greeks and other peoples, one man, Protagoras, worked out a theory which could serve as a defence of democratic systems. A native of Abdera, a small republic on the north coast of the Aegean, Protagoras was roughly a contemporary of Herodotos and Perikles, and like Herodotos he seems to have spent in his maturity a good deal of time in Athens. When in 444, during the time of Perikles' prominence, the Athenians founded a 'model' panhellenic colony, which Herodotos joined, at Thourioi in south Italy, Protagoras was appointed to draw up a code of laws for the new *polis*; unfortunately we know almost nothing about this code, though there is some evidence that there was to be compulsory education at public expense.

Although Plato (c. 429–347), probably following Socrates (469–399), was convinced that the ethical relativism of Protagoras was not a foundation on which a good life for individuals or communities could rest, what he heard from his elders about Protagoras evidently led him to regard the man with considerable respect (and there is reason to think that Aristotle, in dissociating himself to some extent from the doctrines of Plato, was considerably influenced by Protagoras). It is generally thought that the exposition of some of Protagoras' views which Plato puts in his mouth in the dialogue called after him is a fair representation of what Plato believed to be his teaching, for it accords with the little else that we know of him. However, the reference to divine intervention, indeed the whole narrative, was not intended to be taken seriously as an historical account of the rise of civilization; it is a parable.

Plato, *Protagoras* 322–323

Men lived at first in scattered groups; there were no communities. Consequently they got killed by wild beasts, for they were weaker in every respect ... So they sought to save themselves by gathering together and founding communities. But when they had gathered together, they ill-treated one another, since they had not yet acquired the art of citizenship. So they scattered again, and again they faced destruction. Then Zeus, fearing the total destruction of our race, sent Hermes to impart to men the qualities of respect for others and a sense of justice, so that there should be ordered governments and ties of fellow-feeling to draw men together. Hermes asked Zeus in what manner he should bestow these qualities on men. 'Shall I distribute them in the way in which skills have been distributed? What I mean is that one man who possesses medical skill suffices for a large number of laymen, and so with other specialists. Am I to impart these qualities to humanity in the same way, or shall I distribute them to all alike?' 'To all alike,' Zeus replied; 'let everyone have a share, for communities could not exist if few men had a share of these, as they have of other skills. Moreover, lay it down as a law ordained by me that any man who is incapable of taking a share of these qualities is to be put to death, as a plague to the community.'

So for this reason, Socrates, Athenians, like other men, believe that few are capable of giving advice when it is a question of skill in joinery or some other craft; and, as you say, if someone outside those few offers advice, they will not listen—and rightly so, I would say. But when they engage in a discussion involving civic capacity . . ., they rightly listen to everyone, believing that everyone must have a share of civic capacity, otherwise the community could not exist . . .'

Apart from Protagoras, we know of only one major Greek philosopher who came out in clear support of the democratic ideal as beneficial for the whole community: Demokritos (born probably *c.* 460), also a citizen of Abdera, who likewise travelled widely. However, Demokritos seems not to have been involved in the intellectual life of Athens, so probably his experience was of simpler democracies.

Although best known as a natural philosopher, he was a man of wide interests, to judge from the meagre quotations from his writings that have come down to us. Of those on politics we have mere snippets, like a modern newspaper's 'sayings of the week', mostly from an anthology of the fifth century A.D. However, the difference in flavour from the political pronouncements of better-known Greek writers is unmistakable.

Demokritos, *Fragments* 251, 255

Poverty under democracy is as much to be preferred to what is called prosperity under the rule of lords as liberty is to slavery.

When the powerful take it upon themselves to pay taxes for the benefit of the have-nots, to help them, and to show them kindness, there at last you have compassion, the ending of alienation and the attainment of brotherhood; there you have mutual aid, and civic concord, and other benefits too numerous for anyone to list.

THUCYDIDES AND THE PERIKLEAN IDEAL

The best-known encomium on the Athenian political system is contained in the speech which Thucydides (*c.* 455–400) represents Perikles as having delivered at a state funeral in the winter 431–30.

Thucydides 2

34. During the winter the Athenians gave a funeral at public expense to those who had first fallen in the war, this being the traditional

custom... Perikles, the son of Xanthippos, was chosen to give the address..., and he spoke as follows:

36. '... The military achievements to which we owe our power form a part of our history too familiar to my audience for me to enlarge on it, and I shall therefore say nothing about them. There is, however, another subject on which I have something to say before proceeding to my panegyric on these men. What way of life have we followed to reach our present position? To what political system and to what modes of behaviour do we owe our rise to greatness? These are questions to which, I believe, a speaker may properly draw attention on such an occasion as this, questions which this whole gathering, both citizens and foreigners, may consider with advantage.

37. 'Our political system is not modelled on the institutions of neighbouring states; we are rather an example to others than followers of examples that others have set. The name given to it is democracy, since it is based on the majority, not on a small group, but our laws afford equal justice to all in their private differences. As to the estimation in which a man is held in our community, if he distinguishes himself in some sphere he gains preferment, as a rule, on merit, without reference to the class to which he belongs.[3] If on the other hand a man, though poor, has it in him to serve the community in some way, he is not prevented from doing so by the lowliness of his status.

'Freedom is the characteristic feature, not only of our political system but also of our social life. We do not view one another's private pursuits with suspicion, or become indignant about things that our neighbours enjoy doing, or cast sour looks, which, even if they do no real harm, cause distress to those at whom they are directed. But this ease in our private relations does not make us lawless in public life. Fear is our chief safeguard against this: it teaches us to obey both those who hold office and the laws themselves, particularly the laws that exist for the protection of victims of wrongdoing and those unwritten laws which everyone recognizes that a man cannot break without incurring disgrace...

40. 'Wealth is for us something to be used tactfully rather than to be flaunted ostentatiously; poverty is something which one may acknowledge without shame, though it becomes shameful if one does not try to escape from it.

'We succeed in attending to our family affairs without neglecting affairs of state and in having an adequate grasp of political issues even when we are involved in other concerns. For, unlike others, we say of a man who takes no interest in politics, not that he avoids meddling but that he is useless; and while some of us can formulate sound policies, the rest of us can at least assess them soundly. We do not believe that discussion cripples action; we believe that what is really harmful is failure to learn from preliminary discussion before setting out to do what needs to be done.

41. 'In short, I say that our community, taken as a whole, is a school for Greece, and I believe that no one can equal the individual reared in this community in his self-reliant ability to assume the greatest variety of roles and to play them with grace and dexterity...'

'It is remarkable, this aristocratic ideal for the very democratic Athenians —ennobled *petits bourgeois* ... The contrast with the reality is seen most clearly ... in Aristophanes' pictures of the *petits bourgeois*.'*

Are all of Thucydides' words, or any of them, among those that Perikles spoke at that funeral? Opinions differ: but almost all would agree that Thucydides gives us what he believed to have been Perikles' ideas. Perikles seems genuinely to have believed in the People—some would say, because he, like Lenin, was remote from them, an intellectual aristocrat who could not shed his superiority. (There is an interesting parody in Plato's *Menexenos*.) In his time, Athenian political life was in fact balanced on a razor's edge between paternalism and participation.

The Greek republic that probably came nearest, in the fifth century, to Athens in the size of its free population and in its wealth was Syracuse in Sicily; and during much of the century, after a long period of dictatorship, it had a political system formally, at least, similar to that of Athens. In 415, the Athenians sent a large expeditionary force to Sicily in the hope of bringing Syracuse under their control. Thucydides reports a debate in the Assembly at Syracuse on the question of resistance to this invasion.

Thucydides 6

37. Athenagoras, a leader of the People, who at that time exerted a very strong influence over the majority of them, came forward and spoke as follows:

38. '... Not for the first time, I observe that certain persons are trying

* A. W. Gomme, *Historical Commentary on Thucydides* II (1956), 126–7.

to alarm you, the People, so as to get the government into their hands; they have tried to do this on many previous occasions . . . That is why our community is rarely at rest, but is disrupted by constant disturbances and by internal struggles that are as frequent as those against outside enemies, and why it has occasionally succumbed to dictatorship or to the arbitrary rule of a junta. I shall try, if you will support me, to prevent anything of that kind happening in our time . . .

'After all, what is it, I have often asked, that you young men really want? To hold office here and now? The law forbids it, a law which was enacted not to deprive of honour those capable of holding office but because men of your age are not yet capable. You don't like sharing equal rights under law with the great mass of your fellow citizens? But what justification can there be for those who are alike not enjoying the same status?

39. 'Someone will object that democracy is in fact neither sensible nor equitable; those who hold property are the best men to hold office. To this I would say, first, that what democracy means is the rule of the whole People, oligarchy the rule of a section; secondly, that while men of wealth make the most competent custodians of funds, men of intelligence make the most competent councillors and the mass of the People are the best fitted to decide on proposals that are brought forward; and all these sections alike get their due share in a democracy, both individually and taken all together. Oligarchy gives the mass of the People a full share in the risks, but it is not content merely with a larger share of the benefits, it takes and keeps the lot. That is what the young and the influential amongst you are anxious to achieve; but in this great community they can not gain control.'

Soon afterwards, however, Dionysios, a follower of Athenagoras' chief opponent, Hermokrates, transformed the generalship to which he was elected in 406, in the context of war against the Carthaginians, into a dictatorship. Thereafter democracy was never effectively restored (cf. chapter III, p. 76). It is worth asking why it did not take root at Syracuse as it did at Athens.

CONSERVATIVE VIEWS

The natural sympathies of Aristophanes were with country folk, landowners and peasants (who never ceased to constitute a large proportion

Attitudes to Democracy in Greece

of the Athenian citizen body). He did not dislike democracy, recognizing that Athens' greatness was bound up with it, but he thought that leadership should be provided by patriotic members of the old landowning families, rather than by men who had gained enough wealth from some trade to be able to devote themselves to politics, or, worse, and as he seemed to think more probable, men who, not having enough wealth to satisfy them, would be trying to line their pockets at the community's expense. For such men, conscious of not having been born to lead, would flatter and deceive the People and encourage popular fears of alleged enemies at home and abroad in order to retain a hold, for love of power, even if they were not venal; and they would in particular kowtow to the less respectable inhabitants of Athens and the Peiraieus, who could most easily attend sessions of the Assembly and the Courts of Justice. Without ever losing sight of the need to entertain his audience, he felt obliged to warn the Athenians against being bamboozled and exploited by such false friends.

If one remembers that these were his convictions, one can get a better idea of some aspects of life under democracy from him than from any other Greek writer.

In his second surviving play, *Knights*, produced in 424, two slaves (who may have worn masks portraying two leading public figures of the day, Demosthenes and, perhaps, Nikias) are distressed by the hold that a new slave, a Paphlagonian (a cover for the politician Kleon), has succeeded in gaining over their master, Demos—who of course stands for the Athenian People. 'Representation of Kleon as a Paphlagonian is designed to suggest, in accordance with the common forms of political antagonism, that he is not of true Athenian origin, and also to remind us of *paphlásdēn*, "bluster".' * To break the Paphlagonian's hold, they set against him an even more disreputable individual, a sausage-seller. Their efforts are supported by the chorus of Knights (representing the thousand young Athenians who formed the state cavalry—the Knights—a *corps d'élite*, serving with their own horses, which only the wealthiest landowning families could afford to maintain: commoners disliked their long hair and other affectations).

Aristophanes, *Knights* 147–193, 725–755, 1111–1150

Slave: Oh happy sausage-seller! This way, my good friend. 'Arise, thou that art revealed as Athens' saviour.'
Sausage-Seller: What is it? What are you calling me for?

* K. J. Dover, *Aristophanic Comedy*, 89.

Slave: Come here, you lucky man, and let me tell you what a stroke of good fortune you've had.

S.-S.: Why are you making fun of me, mate? Why don't you let me get on with cleaning my offal and selling my sausages?

Slave: Don't worry about offal, you idiot. Look over there. (*Pointing to the audience.*) Do you see those people, row upon row of them?

S.-S.: Yes, I see them.

Slave: You are the liege lord of them all; you are master of the Agora and the docks and the Pnyx as well; you'll trample the Council underfoot, you'll break the Generals, you'll get men arrested and thrown into gaol; you'll have it off in the Town Hall.

S.-S.: Me?

Slave: Yes, you, believe it or not. And that's not all ... (*He goes on to remind the Sausage-Seller of Athens' great power and wealth, which will all be in his hands.*) This oracle here says you're going to be a Very Important Person.[4]

S.-S.: But I ask you, how can I become a V.I.P.? I'm only a sausage-seller.

Slave: That's precisely why you'll become a V.I.P.: because you don't amount to anything, you're from the streets, and you're cheeky.

S.-S.: I don't think I deserve to be so powerful.

Slave: Hell, whatever makes you say you don't deserve to? I suppose you must have a notion that there's some good in you. Were your family people of quality?[5]

S.-S.: Good God no, they didn't amount to anything.

Slave: You lucky man, how well fitted you are for politics!

S.-S.: But I tell you, mate, I haven't got any education. All I can do is read and write, and I'm not too good at that.

Slave: That's the only thing against you, that you can read and write at all. Leading the People isn't a job for an educated man, or a man of good character. You need to be ignorant and disreputable ...

(*The Sausage-Seller has succeeded in winning the Council over to his side. He and the Paphlagonian go on to compete for the favour of Demos.*)

Paphlagonian: (*Knocking on the door of Demos' house*) Demos! come outside!

S.-S.: Please, Dad, do come outside! Dear, sweet Demos!

Paph.: Come and see how dreadfully they're insulting me.

Attitudes to Democracy in Greece

Demos: What's all this shouting? Get away from my door! You've knocked down my harvest decorations. What's wrong, Paphlagonian?
Paph.: On your account I'm beaten up by this man and these kids.
Demos: Why?
Paph.: Because I'm fond of you, Demos, because I'm crazy about you.
Demos: And who are you, may I ask?
S.-S.: I'm his rival. I've been gone on you for a long time, and I've been wanting to do something for you, and so have a lot of other decent honest people. But we can't, because of him. You see, you're like boys with their admirers; you won't pay any attention to good honest people, you give your favours to lamp-merchants and cobblers and shoemakers and tanners.
Paph.: That's because I'm kind to Demos.
S.-S.: I ask you, in what way? . . .
Paph.: Go ahead, Demos, and hold an Assembly, so that you can tell which of us is your best friend. Choose between us.
S.-S.: Yes, by all means choose between us—but not on the Pnyx!
Paph.: I wouldn't hold a session anywhere else. Let's go, then. We must meet on the Pnyx.
S.-S.: Blast, that's my cursed luck; that's the finish of me. The old man is as clever as they come when he's at home, but when he's sitting on that stony hillside he's as dozy as if he were packing figs in boxes.

(*During a break in the contest, the chorus of Knights have their say—giving Aristophanes the opportunity to state his true view of the People—or at least to remove any offence he may have given.*)

Knights: Power's a fine thing to have, Demos, when people all fear you as they would a despot. All the same, it's easy to lead you by the nose: you love to be flattered and fooled; you gape at every speaker in turn; your mind wanders while you're sitting there.
Demos: There's not much of a mind under that long hair of yours, if you believe that I have no sense. I play the simpleton on purpose. I enjoy having my daily needs looked after, and so I like to keep one man to protect me, even if he is a thief. But when he's had his fill, I grab hold of him and bash him.
Knights: Good luck to you, then, if there's as much cunning in your simple-mindedness as you say—if you purposely fatten your public

victims on the Pnyx and then choose the plumpest to sacrifice and dine off when you happen to need something to make a meal.

Demos: Just watch how skilfully I trap types who fancy that they're being clever and fooling me. I have my eye on them all the time, and I watch them lining their pockets, although I seem not to notice. In the end I make them cough up everything they've pinched from me by sticking the funnel of the ballot-box down their throats.

The contest ends with Demos making the Sausage-Seller his steward in place of the Paphlagonian. 'Many elements in the play seem designed to promote a sentimental unity of classes against leaders like Kleon . . . It may well seem that having chosen one end of the social scale for the chorus of *Knights* Aristophanes deliberately emphasizes its community of interests with the other end.' * Here, then, we have an attitude very different from that of the Old Oligarch (chapter III), writing at almost the same time. This may mean that it is a mistake to regard Aristophanes as standing on 'the right'; or it may serve to remind us that in Athens, as in other democracies, neither 'the right' nor 'the left' speaks with a single voice—or, as some might prefer to say, speaks with the same voice to different audiences.

In trying to show that the teaching of Socrates had not been politically subversive, as people alleged, Xenophon, who himself had the conservative outlook of a country gentleman and army officer, but who had been deeply impressed in his youth by Socrates' goodness, is led into telling an anecdote about Alkibiades and Perikles which one may hesitate to regard as historical but which no doubt faithfully reflects some of the discussion that went on about democracy and the rule of law.

Xenophon, *Memoirs* 1.2

I find it astonishing also that some people were convinced that Socrates corrupted the young . . . What his accuser alleged was that he made those who associated with him despise the established laws, by arguing that it was foolish to appoint holders of public office by lot: no one would employ a man chosen by lot as a helmsman or a joiner or a flautist or for any other such job, although mistakes made in such jobs do much less harm than mistakes in government. Talk of that

---

* Dover, *Aristophanic Comedy*, 99.

Attitudes to Democracy in Greece

kind, his accuser said, encouraged the young to regard the established order with contempt and to be ready to use violence ... He pointed to the fact that two of Socrates' associates, Kritias and Alkibiades, did Athens the greatest possible harm. Kritias became the most violent and insatiable of all the members of the oligarchic junta,[6] while under the democracy there was no one as wild and outrageous as Alkibiades.

Well, I shall not try to excuse any harm that these two did to Athens; I shall simply explain the nature of their association with Socrates. The fact is that they were the two most ambitious Athenians of their time; they wanted to be in control of everything and to become more celebrated than anyone ... Their aim in associating with Socrates was, I believe, to acquire the maximum efficiency as speakers and as men of action ..., and as soon as they had become superior, in their own estimation, to the other members of his circle, they broke away from him and went in for politics, which had been their aim from the outset ... Even while they were still associating with Socrates, the people with whom they were most anxious to converse were those most active in politics. There is, for instance, a story that when Alkibiades was not yet twenty he had a conversation along the following lines with Perikles, who was his guardian as well as being a leading politician.

'Tell me, Perikles, can you explain to me what law is?'

'Why, yes, certainly I can,' Perikles replied.

'Then please do explain,' said Alkibiades. 'I hear people being praised for being law-abiding, and I don't think anyone deserves such praise unless he knows what law is.'

'Well now, that isn't a difficult wish to gratify, Alkibiades, your wanting to know what law is. Whenever the People meet en masse and put in writing a statement laying down what must and must not be done, that constitutes a law.' ...

'But supposing that those who meet and issue a statement about what should be done are not the mass of the People but a minority, as happens under an oligarchy, what will that be?'

'Every statement about what should be done that is published, after due deliberation, by the controlling body of a state is called a law.'

'So, if a dictator is in control of a state and issues a statement to the citizens about what they must do, that too is law?'

'Yes, when there is a dictatorship, every order that the dictator publishes is likewise called a law.'

'But what about constraint, Perikles? Isn't it the negation of law if someone stronger uses force rather than persuasion to make someone weaker do whatever he thinks fit?'

'That is my opinion,' said Perikles.

'And if a dictator issues statements requiring people to do things without having gained their consent, that constitutes the negation of law?'

'I agree,' said Perikles. 'I take back what I said just now, that orders which a dictator issues constitute law if he has not gained the people's consent.'

'And what about orders issued by a minority when it is in control, without the consent of the majority? Does that constitute constraint?'

'In my view,' said Perikles, 'if anyone compels someone to obey orders, written or spoken, without having gained his consent, that constitutes constraint rather than law.'

'So, if the broad mass of the People have the upper hand over the owners of property and issue orders without having gained their consent, will that constitute constraint rather than law?'

'We used to be terribly clever at that kind of thing, Alkibiades, when we were your age,' Perikles is said to have replied. 'We went in for the sort of ingenious arguing that you evidently go in for now.'

'I wish I had known you, Perikles, when you were at your cleverest.'

So, as soon as Alkibiades and Kritias thought that they could get the better of the politicians, they gave up Socrates' company . . .

Another point that his accuser made was that he selected the most mischievous passages from the works of the most admired poets and used them to support his case, in teaching those who associated with him to be vicious and domineering . . . According to him, Socrates constantly quoted the passage from Homer (*Iliad* 2, 188–202) in which Odysseus, 'whenever he met a prince or a man of eminence, stood beside him and restrained him with gentle words: "Sir, it becomes you not to spread alarm alike a coward. Instead, be seated, and make the rest of the folk sit down . . ." But when he saw a man of the people and caught him bawling, he struck him with his staff and uttered words of rebuke: "Sir, keep still, and listen to what your betters have to say. Weak and unwarlike as you are, you will never count, either in war or in debate."' This, it was said, he interpreted to mean that the poet approved of the beating of commoners and poor men.

Attitudes to Democracy in Greece

But Socrates did not say that. If he had, he would have been suggesting that he ought to be beaten himself. What he did say was that those who neither did nor said anything useful, who were incapable of giving any assistance, either to the army or to the state or to the People themselves, if need arose, should be placed under every kind of restraint, especially if they were self-assertive into the bargain, even if they should happen to be quite rich. Socrates himself was just the opposite: he was manifestly a friend of the People, and well disposed to all mankind.

THE ATTITUDE OF THE RICH

In several speeches written for delivery in Court by wealthy Athenians charged during the early years of the fourth century with crimes against the state, Lysias (*c.* 459–380) presents the attitude of such persons to the democratic system, or at least the attitude which he thought it expedient and plausible for them to profess. One such speech has been quoted already in chapter I; here is part of another.

Lysias 25.1–3, 7–14

I do not blame you, gentlemen, for feeling equally indignant with all who remained in town (*under the arbitrary rule of the Thirty*), after listening to such a speech and being reminded of those events; but I am astonished that my prosecutors, men who neglect their own concerns to attend to those of others, and who know quite well the difference between those who did no harm and those who committed numerous offences, endeavour to persuade you to adopt a hostile attitude to all of us ...

If they have brought these events up on the ground that they have something to do with me, I shall prove that they are telling a pack of lies and that I behaved in the way in which the best of those in the resistance movement would have behaved if they had remained in town. I beseech you, gentlemen, not to share the attitude of professional prosecutors. It is their job to bring charges even against people who have committed no offence, for they can make most money out of such people; but it is your duty to allow those who do no harm to enjoy an equal share of political rights; for that is how you will get the widest possible support for the established order ...

I shall endeavour to explain to you which citizens, in my view, are likely to favour oligarchy and which democracy. This will show you, and I shall be presenting my own defence in showing you, that there is nothing in what I have done, either under democracy or under oligarchy, to make it likely that I would be disloyal to the mass of the citizen body.

To begin with, you should bear in mind that no human being is naturally oligarchic or naturally democratic: everyone gives his support to the political order that serves his interests. So it largely rests with you to ensure that the existing system enjoys the widest possible support. Examples from past history can teach you that this is so. For consider, gentlemen, how often the champions of both systems changed sides. Have you forgotten that Phrynichos and Peisandros and the popular leaders associated with them brought into power the first of the two oligarchic régimes (*May–September 411, when the whole government was carried on by a Council of Four Hundred*), because they were afraid of being punished for the offences they had committed against you; and that many who had served in the Council of Four Hundred under that régime returned to Athens with the men of the Peiraieus (*where the movement which ousted the Thirty had its base*); while some of those who helped to oust the Four Hundred turned round and became members of the Thirty? ...

It is easy, then, gentlemen, to see that the differences that arise between people have to do, not with political systems, but with their individual personal interests. This, then, is what you should bear in mind in conducting examinations of citizens: you should consider what part they played in civic life under democracy, and ask whether they derived any benefit from a change of régime; that is how you will form the fairest judgement.

I therefore hold that persons who under democracy lost their civic rights after investigation of their conduct as office-holders, or were deprived of their property or experienced some other such misfortune, are likely to favour a change of system, hoping that this will be advantageous to themselves; but that those who have conferred many benefits on the People and have done no harm whatsoever at any time—men who deserve to be thanked for what they have done instead of being put on trial—should not be allowed by you to become victims of slander, not even if all those active in public life insist that they are oligarchic.

In my case, gentlemen, nothing unpleasant ever happened in public or in private in those days to make me desire a change as a means of escaping from a nasty situation. I served five times as captain of a warship, I contributed to capital levies on many occasions during the war, and I performed other public services as well as any citizen. Indeed, I spent more than the state required, my object being to acquire a better reputation in your eyes, so that, if anything unpleasant ever happened to me, I should be in a stronger position on coming up for trial.

Under oligarchy I was deprived of all these advantages, for the régime's favour was not bestowed on those who had been in one way or another benefactors of the mass of citizens; the persons appointed to office were those who had done you the most harm, for whom you had thus provided the requisite credentials.

All of you should bear these points in mind and should disbelieve the prosecution's allegations, judging every individual by his actions. I was not one of the Four Hundred, gentlemen—let any of my accusers step forward and prove it if he can. Again, after the Thirty came to power, no one can produce evidence of my having served as a Councillor or having held any office whatsoever. If, then, I had the opportunity but declined, I deserve your respect; if on the other hand those in power did not consider me suitable to participate in their régime, what clearer proof could there be that my accusers are lying?

Isokrates (*c.* 436–338) was the son of a rich Athenian and had an expensive education, studying under Gorgias amongst others; but his family lost much of their wealth during the Peloponnesian War, and after the end of the war, he, like Lysias, took to writing speeches for others to deliver in Court. Before long, however, he founded a rhetorical school, which became extremely influential and remunerative. From 380 onwards he published a series of pamphlets, in the form of speeches or letters, which served as samples of his technique but also contained political advice.

In a pamphlet published in about 355 he urged the Athenians to modify the democratic system, giving large supervisory powers to the Council of the Areopagus, which under full democracy had retained only a few functions, mostly of a religious nature; the pamphlet is therefore known as *Areopagiticus*.

Isokrates, *Areopagiticus*

16. I have come to the conclusion that our only hope of averting the dangers that threaten us and of escaping from our present troubles lies in restoring the democracy for which Solon, the People's best friend, created the legal framework, the democracy which was re-established by Kleisthenes when he ousted the despots and brought the People back into power. Nothing could be devised that would be more favourable to the People or more beneficial to Athens . . .

20. Those who governed the state in those days did not create a régime that was called by the most impartial and disarming of names only to seem to those who came into contact with it not to be in practice of that character. It was not a régime that trained the citizens to think that democracy means permissiveness, that liberty connotes defiance of the law, that equality of rights entitles one to speak as one pleases and that happiness depends on the toleration of such conduct. On the contrary, it abhorred people with such ideas and kept them under control, and it made all the citizens better and more self-disciplined.

What contributed most to the good management of the state was that people did not fail to realize which was the more serviceable of the two prevailing notions of equality—giving everyone equal shares, and giving each man his due. They rejected as wrong the idea of according the same rights to men of worth and men who were good for nothing, choosing instead to award preferment, and punishment, to each man according to his deserts. It was on that principle that they ran the state. Thus in filling offices they did not draw lots among the citizens at large; instead they had a preliminary election to pick out the best men and those most capable of performing the various functions . . . They believed that this arrangement was more to the People's advantage than appointment by lot; for when lots are cast chance is the judge, and offices would often go, they thought, to partisans of oligarchy, whereas preliminary selection of the most suitable candidates would enable the People to choose those most attached to the established order . . .

26. To sum up, their verdict was that the People must have absolute control over the appointment of officials, the punishment of offenders and the settlement of disputes, but that those who could afford leisure, having adequate means, should attend as servants of the People to matters of common concern. If they behaved justly, they should be

thanked, and with that recognition they should be content, but if they mismanaged things no mercy was to be shown them; they should be subject to the severest penalties. How could one have a more stable or a more just democracy than one which sets the ablest men to govern but puts the People in control of them?

70. ... In what I have been saying I have had two aims: first, to show that what I myself favour is not oligarchy or any régime that gives anyone more than his due, but a just and orderly political system; secondly, that democracies, even if they are ill organized, cause less misfortune, while if they are well constituted they have the merit of being more just, more impartial and more agreeable to live under.

(*This will, I hope, explain*) my object in urging you to modify a system that has so many splendid achievements to its credit, and why I have at one moment been singing the praises of democracy, while at the next moment I turn around and utter criticisms and complaints about existing arrangements ...

The idea expressed here by Isokrates and a few years later by Aristotle (see chapter I, pp. 36f.), that there are two different kinds of equality, makes its first appearance in surviving literature as a political concept in the first half of the fourth century, in an earlier work by Isokrates and before that, implicitly, in Plato's *Gorgias*. 'It may well be the Pythagorean answer to the democratic slogan of "equality"'; * for those who regarded themselves as disciples of Pythagoras, the sixth-century thinker who had a strong influence on Plato, were in favour of aristocracy.

The idea was subsequently taken up by others who believed, and wanted to give intellectual respectability to the belief, that some men deserve a larger share of power than others. However, some of them felt obliged to concede, whether forthrightly, like Aristotle, or halfheartedly, like Cicero, that those who happened to own more property were not necessarily the men who deserved a larger share of power.

As Isokrates hints, getting 'back to Kleisthenes' would have meant not only reviving the supervisory powers of the Council of the Areopagus but also reverting to the election of archons (though he seems to prefer a mixed system, choice by lot between elected candidates), reimposing a high property qualification for office and abolishing payment for the performance of civic functions: which would, of course, have affected the People's 'absolute control' of the Courts.

In a pamphlet, *On the Peace*, probably published shortly before *Areopagiticus*, just after the Athenians had experienced a serious setback in

* E. R. Dodds, *Plato: Gorgias* 339.

their attempts to regain hegemony in the Aegean, and at about the time of Xenophon's pamphlet *Ways and Means* (chapter III), Isokrates, in giving them advice on foreign policy, found occasion to make some other comments on the democratic system.

Isokrates, *On the Peace*

52. Experienced though we are both in discussion and in action, we are so irrational that we do not hold the same opinions on the same subject for a single day. On the contrary, the policies that we criticize before going to the Assembly are the policies for which we raise our hands when we are in session; but not long afterwards, on leaving the meeting, we criticize the resolutions for which we voted.

We claim to be the cleverest of the Greeks, but we turn for advice to men who are beneath contempt; and we put these same men in charge of all the community's affairs, although no one would trust them with any of his private business...

64. It is maritime power that has thrown us into our present chaos, and that put an end to democracy of the sort that made our ancestors who lived under it the most fortunate of the Greeks.

ATHENIANS AND OTHER GREEKS: LIBERATION OR TYRANNY?

Isokrates' remarks on the Athenians' attachment to naval power may serve to remind us that in many other Greek states, particularly between the middle of the fifth century and the middle of the fourth, attitudes to democracy were complicated by the fact that the Athenian People had in the fifth century reduced most of the other states of the Aegean to tributary status, and in the fourth century they were suspected of aspiring to reassert Athenian overlordship.

There were clearly many states in which most of the commons favoured democracy and welcomed the Athenian connection. There were probably, however, some states in which a desire for democracy was a less potent motive, even among quite ordinary people, than dislike of Athenian meddling and high-handedness. Thucydides goes so far as to say this of Greece at large, at the outbreak of the Peloponnesian War in 431:

People were much more sympathetic with the Spartans, especially as they proclaimed that they would liberate Greece... The majority were strongly anti-Athenian, some because they wanted to throw off Athenian control, others for fear of being subjected to it. (2.8)

But his subsequent narrative of the war does not justify this statement, accurately though it reflects, no doubt, the impression he formed at the time. What we do find is that men's attitudes were further confused at places and times at which Athens' enemies were gaining the upper hand.

In 428, for instance, the state of Mytilene, on the island of Lesbos, which had an oligarchic régime, repudiated its (non-tributary) alliance with the Athenians, on the ground that, having entered into alliance fifty years earlier for protection from the Persians and to take reprisals from them, it now found itself drawn into war against Athens' enemies in Greece. The Athenians sent a force against Mytilene; and in 427, after the oligarchs had distributed arms to the people, the people compelled the government to surrender to the Athenians, Peloponnesian help promised to the oligarchs having failed to arrive. The Athenian Assembly then considered how this disloyal state should be treated. At first the People decided that all the adult males should be killed and the women and children sold as slaves; but the next day the question was reopened. Kleon advised adherence to the decision, but Diodotos urged that only the organizers should be put on trial, and his proposal was adopted. Thucydides has reported his arguments, all based on considerations of expediency. What he is made to say in the following passage was largely borne out by subsequent events elsewhere.

Thucydides 3.47

Consider what a serious mistake you would be making in another respect, too, if you were to follow Kleon's advice. As things are now, the people in every community are sympathetic towards you; and they either do not join the minority in schemes for secession or, if they are forced to do so, are opposed from the outset to those who are seceding, so that you go to war with the great majority of the opposing community on your side. However, if you destroy the Mytilenean people, who took no part in the secession and who willingly surrendered as soon as they got hold of arms, for one thing you will be doing wrong in putting to death men who have done you a service and secondly you will be creating the very situation that the influential elements most desire; for in organizing the secession of their states they will have the people on their side from the outset, since you will have shown in advance that the same punishment is in store for those who have done wrong and those who have not. Even if in this instance they had done wrong, we must avoid turning our only remaining allies into enemies.

That Diodotos (or Thucydides) could refer in this fashion to the mass of the populace in the various states, as 'our only remaining allies', reflects the continuing hold of the old ruling classes over men's imaginations—and over other instruments of power.

In 411 Alkibiades, who had fallen out with the Spartans, with whom he had found refuge after getting into trouble at Athens, sent messages to certain influential Athenians who were serving with the Athenian fleet at Samos. He told them that if they could bring about an oligarchic revolution at Athens, and his rehabilitation, he could persuade Tissaphernes, the Persian governor of western Asia Minor, with whom he was staying, to stop subsidizing Athens' enemies and to subsidize Athens instead. Thucydides tells us the result.

Thucydides 8.48

They brought some suitable people into a conspiracy, and they declared openly to the main body of the fleet that the King would come over to their side and provide subsidies if Alkibiades returned and democracy was abolished. Although the sailors' immediate reaction was to resent what was going on, the prospect of getting pay from the King made them hold their peace.[7]

After the organizers of the plan for oligarchy had given this information to the fleet, they held further discussions among themselves and with their sympathizers about Alkibiades' proposals. Most of them thought that they could count on everything going smoothly, but Phrynichos, who was still a General, did not like the plan at all.

He objected that Alkibiades cared no more for oligarchy than he did for democracy (which was true), and that all that he was after was to find a way of changing the existing régime and getting himself recalled by those on the opposite side . . . As for the allied states, to which they were promising oligarchy, because, it was said, Athens itself was to cease to be a democracy, he was quite sure, he declared, that this would not make those that had seceded return to their allegiance or those that remained any more reliable; for rather than remain subject to Athens, whether under oligarchy or under democracy, they would prefer to be free under whatever régime they might happen to have. They did not imagine that the so-called men of quality [8] would make things any less unpleasant for them than the People had, for it had been men of quality who had supplied the People with ideas for oppressing Athens' subjects, mainly for their own benefit. If they were to be wholly at the mercy of such men, they would find themselves condemned to death without trial and in a more arbitrary fashion, whereas the People had been their refuge and had kept men of that kind under control. He was quite convinced, he said, that this was the state of opinion in the allied states, which had learnt by bitter experience. So far as he was concerned, he did not approve of the negotiations with Alkibiades or of any of the things that were currently being done.

Thucydides admired Phrynichos' good judgment, as he tells us elsewhere. But this advice was disregarded by the conspirators.

In the fourth century, the Spartans tried for a time to exercise hegemony outside the Peloponnese, their traditional sphere; but people found them even more overbearing than the Athenians—and Athens was much weaker. So on the one hand opportunists had little hope of gaining advantage for themselves by espousing the democratic cause within their communities; but on the other hand there was no longer any need, generally speaking, for others to feel torn between sympathy with democracy and love of freedom, especially as the chief threat to freedom, after the eclipse of Sparta, was not from any democratic Greek state but from the Kings of Persia and Macedon.

MAKING THE BEST OF THINGS

It is therefore somewhat ironic that the fullest study of the *polis* and the most objective analysis of democracy were made by a man employed for a time by Philip of Macedon to tutor his heir, Alexander: Aristotle. What we have from Aristotle does not, however, constitute a coherent treatment. It has come down to us in a collection of material which he left at his death in varying stages of elaboration, the collection which we know as his *Politics*: a much less seductive work than the *Republic* of Plato, his one-time teacher, whose brilliant caricature of democracy (8.557–561) is so familiar that it has been omitted here. There is no room here to give more than a little of what Aristotle has to say—his treatment, for example, of citizenship in Book 3 and of individual democracies in Books 5 and 6 has had perforce to be left out—but from what follows we can see that he was torn between the interest that he shared with his master, Plato, in determining how society should ideally be organized, to enable men to rise to the height of their potentialities, and a desire to find out and explain what could be done to improve the arrangements that actually existed in the *poleis* of his day. So we find him analysing and assessing the attitudes and the demands of various social groups and considering how in particular cases these might be reconciled.

Aristotle, *Politics* 5.1

Democracy is based on the idea that those who are equal in some respect are absolutely equal: people imagine that all who are alike in being free men are absolutely equal; oligarchy is based on the idea that those who are unequal in some one respect are altogether unequal: people suppose that those who are unequal in wealth are unequal absolutely. Some then claim an equal share in everything on the ground that they are equal; others endeavour to get more on the ground that they are not equal, for an unequal share means a larger share. Both have some right on their side, but both make the mistake of oversimplifying.

Politics 6.4

The establishment of democracy is acceptable wherever the masses live by agriculture or by stockbreeding. For the fact that they do not possess much wealth keeps them busy, so that they seldom meet in Assembly . . . The power to elect officials and to investigate their conduct in office satisfies their requirements, in so far as they do want to count for something . . .

With a political system of this kind government is bound to be good; for the offices will always be in the hands of the best citizens, but with the consent of the People, who will therefore not feel resentment towards men of the better sort. The notables will be satisfied with this arrangement, for they will not be governed by their inferiors; but they will govern justly, because others have the power to call them to account. It is good for men to be dependent on others and not be able to do whatever they think fit; for, if one has freedom to do whatever one likes, there is nothing to keep in check one's evil impulses . . .

Other democracies have as their constituent mass people who are as a rule of far poorer quality, for they live poor lives; there is nothing of moral value in any of the work done by those in menial occupations and shopkeepers and labourers. What makes matters worse is that people of this kind, being constantly in town and around the market place, can easily attend an Assembly . . .

Politics 5.9

In those democracies that are supposed to be the most favourable to the people a wrong notion of liberty prevails. There are two things that are thought to be the marks of democracy: liberty and sovereignty of the majority; for the democratic notion of justice is equality, and equality means that what the masses decide is final, while liberty means that anyone can do what he likes. Consequently, in democracies of this kind everyone lives as he pleases—'following his fancy', as Euripides puts it. This is frivolous: to live in harmony with the system should give one a sense of security, not of servitude.

Aristotle does not entertain the idea, which in this century has been so eloquently presented by Rosa Luxemburg, for instance, that participation will itself engender *politike arete*, the qualities appropriate to a citizen. Nor has he any sympathy with the liberal ideal of 'reserving a large area of private life', within which a man can do as he pleases: * 'this is frivolous'.

There were, he implies, some states in which 'everyone lives as he pleases'; but (despite what Thucydides makes Perikles say of the Athenians) the prosecution of Socrates, for instance, shows that there were limits, and that Aristotle was not altogether out of line with ordinary Greek opinion. It was not, however, a question of the individual being subjected to the tyranny of the state; there was no conflict in the Greek world between the state and the individual, for the citizens were the state. What the individual was up against was the pressure to conform that is exerted in any small, close-knit community; but probably very few had the sense of being up against it.

In holding that freedom to do as one pleases is 'a wrong notion of liberty', Aristotle was in agreement with Plato. But we have seen that, unlike Plato, he did not wholly condemn democracy, and was even pre-

* See Isaiah Berlin, *Four Essays on Liberty* (1969) lviiff, 122ff.

pared to concede that control by the People might help to make 'the notables' govern justly. There remains one other passage in which he goes beyond recognizing that democracy is an unavoidable necessity in certain circumstances and acknowledges that it may have positive merits.

Politics 3.11

That the masses should be in control rather than the best men, since the best are few, is a view that some would appear to hold; and, although it raises difficulties, there may also be some truth in it. For even if no one individual from among the masses is up to much, it is possible that, when they get together, they may be superior to the few, not individually but collectively, in the same way that feasts to which all contribute are better than those given at one man's expense. For, where there are many people, each has some share of ability and intelligence, and when they get together they become as it were one multiple man with many feet and hands and sense-organs; so too as regards character and intellect. That is why the many are better judges of works of music and poetry; some appreciate some parts, some others, but collectively they appreciate the work as a whole ... Furthermore, a large number is less corruptible ... When an individual is overcome by anger or by some other such passion, his judgement is inevitably corrupted; but it is difficult to make a whole mass of people get into a passion and go wrong ...

These considerations enable us to answer the question, who and what should be under the control of the mass of free men—those, that is to say, who are not wealthy and who have no claim whatever to excellence. It is unsafe to have them sharing in the highest offices, for their foolishness and their indifference to justice will lead them into mistakes and crimes; but on the other hand it is dangerous to deny them any opportunity to participate, for a state in which there are many poor men who are excluded from participation is bound to be full of enemies.

Politics 6.3

It is always the weaker who seek after equality and justice; those who are in power do not care at all.

V. Democracy and Empire: Alexander and After

KINGS AND REPUBLICS

After Alexander the Great, building on the achievements of his father, Philip, had made himself master of the whole of the civilized world from the Adriatic to India, most Greek *poleis* remained under the control of one or other of the kings, Macedonian or native, who ruled various parts of what had been Alexander's empire. Most of these *poleis* adopted, or retained, democratic political institutions broadly similar to those of Athens; for most of the kings felt it to be in their interest to support democracy, following the example of Alexander, who in invading Asia Minor and liberating the Greek *poleis* there from Persian rule 'ordered the oligarchies everywhere to be abolished and democracies to be set up' (Arrian, *The Campaigns of Alexander* 1.18). However, Alexander left petty dictators in control if it suited his convenience, and some oligarchies crept back; and new cities that the kings founded, such as Antioch, often had more authoritarian government with no element of democracy.

In the democracies of this age the People were, of course, still an élite, coexisting with a population of outsiders. Everywhere there were slaves and ex-slaves, and aliens who, or whose forebears, had chosen for one reason or another to immigrate. But in states that lay outside the frontiers of modern Greece there were often also indigenous inhabitants, who might be serfs or might, though free, be excluded from any share in the running of the *polis*. There were also sometimes soldiers who were in the employ of some king (or of the *polis* itself), installed as a garrison; or ex-service men who had been settled on royal land adjacent to the territory of the *polis*, or on land within the *polis* which the king had acquired for that purpose. The question could arise of granting citizenship to some section of outsiders, and this could have a bearing on the character of a democracy (as Aristotle had seen), although probably most of those given citizenship in this age were more interested in the status or the socio-economic advantages that it gave them than in political participation.

What we do not know is how large a part ordinary citizens played in the political life of these democracies, since official documents seldom reveal such things, nor do they fall within the range of interest of most writers of or on this period whose work survives. But it is reasonable to conjecture that generally there was 'a tacit convention whereby the People elected rich men to magistracies and they as magistrates contributed freely to the public services under their charge' * (magistrates being what we have elsewhere called office-holders).

A document containing a decree passed by the People of the Aegean island state of Samos early in the second century shows, as do many others, that the forms, at least, of popular participation were still observed. It also shows what substantial benefits the People of a relatively prosperous *polis* might secure for themselves if and in so far as the rich thought it prudent to cooperate. It lays down arrangements for the investment of money contributed voluntarily by rich citizens and for the use of the income for annual purchases of grain, to be distributed in free rations to all the citizens. The opening is lost, but it is clear from what follows that the first paragraph was concerned with the election of a Board of Trustees to manage the investments.

W. Dittenberger, *Sylloge Inscriptionum Graecarum* (3rd edn, 1922), no. 976

... from among the wealthiest citizens. They shall be appointed at the second meeting of the Assembly in the month Kronion. The Assembly shall be convened in the Theatre by the Presiding Committee, who shall instruct those attending to sit by Thousands, having first put up signs and marked out a place for each of the Thousands.[1] Anyone who disobeys and fails to sit with his Thousand shall be fined a traditional stater.[2] If he declares that he has been wrongly fined, he shall submit a complaint and the matter shall be adjudicated in the Civic Court of Justice within twenty days. Candidates shall be nominated by members of their own Thousand, who shall vote on them by show of hands ... (*The decree proceeds to set forth in detail the duties of the Trustees, of an elected Grain Board of Two who are to buy and distribute the grain, and of an elected Grain Commissioner, who may be required to use surplus funds to purchase further grain.*)

The members of the Grain Board ... are to distribute all the grain that has been bought to the citizens then present in Samos, Thousand by Thousand, measuring out for each citizen two measures per month,

* A. H. M. Jones, *The Greek City from Alexander to Justinian* (1940), 167.

free of charge. They are to commence the distribution in the month Pelusion and continue for as many months as the supply holds out . . . (*The decree goes on to give further details of the distribution procedure, and to prescribe penalties for anyone who fails to fulfil his official duties or his financial obligations.*) No one shall be permitted to spend any of the money or of the interest on it on any thing other than the grain that is to be distributed free of charge. If any member of the Presiding Committee puts on the agenda, or if any speaker proposes, or if any Chairman puts to the vote, any proposal that the money should be used for any other purpose or transferred to any other fund, he shall be fined ten thousand drachmas; so also if a Treasurer or a Trustee or a member of the Grain Board or a Grain Commissioner hands over or uses the money for any other purpose than for grain to be distributed free of charge.

FEDERATION AND REPRESENTATIVE DEMOCRACY

The only writer of this period who tells us much about democracy is Polybios, a Greek historian. Writing in the second century, he inserted into his narrative at one point a generalized picture of monarchy degenerating into tyranny, and being then succeeded by aristocracy (rule by those best qualified) which itself degenerates into oligarchy (rule by a wealthy minority), and is then succeeded by democracy, which degenerates into ochlocracy (mob-rule), which is followed by a reversion to monarchy. He asserts that 'this is the regular cycle of political systems'; but his account probably owes less to observation than to borrowings from books written by philosophers from Plato onwards; mainly, perhaps, from second-rate popular works, lost to us, written nearer his own time. That is to say, it probably tells us more about Polybios' education, interacting with his class prejudices, than it does about Greek democracy in the third and second centuries.

Of greater value for the study of democratic realities and ideas among the Greeks of his time is an earlier passage in which he speaks with enthusiasm of the 'true democracy' that had been achieved by his own state, the Achaian Confederacy, in whose political life he himself played an important part, as a member of one of its wealthiest families. This was a federal union of a large number of *poleis* in southern Greece, mostly within the Peloponnese, which were thus enabled to retain a more substantial freedom vis-à-vis the great monarchies than individual *poleis* could enjoy, but without sacrifice of the political life of the individual *polis*. A number of other such confederacies were in existence within the Greek world at this time, but it became the largest.

Polybios 2

37. A few words should be said at this point about the earlier history of the Achaian nation. As I have already remarked, the Achaians have experienced in our time an astonishing increase in strength and solidarity. In the past there have been numerous attempts to promote unity in the Peloponnese, but none have succeeded, the reason being that the aim of those concerned has been the aggrandisement of their own states rather than universal liberty. In our time, however, the cause of unity has made tremendous progress and has scored notable achievements: not only a cordial agreement on joint defence but also a common legal code and common weights, measures and currency; and in addition a federal government, comprising officials, Councillors and a Court of Justice. What it amounts to is that almost the whole of the Peloponnese has assumed the character of a single republic. The only difference is that there is not a single fortified enclosure serving all the inhabitants; otherwise they all have identical, or similar, institutions, collectively and within their separate states.

38. We may usefully begin by considering how the name Achaian came to cover all the inhabitants of the Peloponnese. The territory occupied by those who have traditionally borne this name since the earliest times is not extensive, nor do they possess a great number of towns, or exceptional wealth, or outstanding ability. The Arkadians have a considerably larger population and territory; so do the Lakonians;[3] and these peoples have always been second to none of the other Greeks in their soldierly qualities. How and why has it come about that they, and the rest of the Peloponnesians, are proud to have acquired a share in the Achaian political system and the right to call themselves Achaians?...

In my opinion, the explanation is that the institutions and principles of equality of rights and freedom of speech and true democracy in general are not to be found exemplified more genuinely anywhere than in the political system which the Achaians have created. Some of the Peloponnesians chose voluntarily to adopt this system; persuasive arguments brought in many others. Occasionally some were forced to join, but those that were compelled soon came to take pride in it. That is because no advantage was reserved for the original members; new members were given completely equal rights. Thus progress was rapid, aided by the most powerful of stimulants, equality and generosity. This political system, then, must be regarded as the source and cause of the prosperity that the Peloponnesians, living in harmony, now enjoy ...

42. I have gone back over past history, first in order to show how and in what circumstances and on whose initiative, among the original Achaians, the foundations of the present system were laid, and secondly to provide empirical backing for my assertions about the political principles of the Achaians. For they have adhered throughout to the principle of offering to others the equality of rights and the freedom of speech that they themselves enjoy. They have warred and struggled continuously against those who, relying either on their own resources or on the help of the Kings, have sought to enslave their own fatherlands. In this way and on the basis of this policy they have achieved success in their undertaking, partly by their own efforts, partly by those of their allies. They have never sought to turn any of their successes to their own selfish advantage; their reward for their efforts has been to achieve freedom for each individual community and harmony throughout the Peloponnese.

This is the only description of the Achaian Confederacy that we possess. There are numerous references to its activities elsewhere in Polybios' history, in other historical works, and in documents; but there is much that we do not know about how the government functioned, especially as there were evidently considerable changes during the period 280–146, to which most of the evidence relates. It is, however, clear that the organs of federal government were formally parallel to those of the traditional *polis*: that is to say, in addition to a Council, with hundreds of members and a number of officials, there was an Assembly; but 'the extent of the League territory ... meant that the Assembly seldom met and that even the Council did not sit permanently. That made the position of the officials all the stronger; thus there was an almost complete reversal of the *polis* constitution.' * Moreover, 'beside the leading board' of officials—known as *Damiurgoi*, workers for the People—'which could be regarded as a smaller Council, stood a single man, the *Strategos*, as the leader in war and often enough in politics too. He was the decisive leader of the executive.' *

* Victor Ehrenberg, *The Greek State* (1969), 126.

In modern terms one could call this a representative democracy of a presidential type, but with a participating element; for every adult male citizen had the right to attend the Assembly (which had to be called to decide on issues of peace and war) as well as the right to stand for office. The number of Councillors elected by each member state seems to have been in proportion to its population, and in the Assembly each state probably had a corresponding number of votes, so that, although those who turned up determined how their state's votes were cast, those who lived in the state in which the Assembly met could not dominate the voting.

In principle, then, a democracy. And, although the word *demokratia* was perhaps already beginning to be used in a loose way in Polybios' time, to cover any constitutional régime, Polybios did not use it thus. Whenever he spoke of democracy, he meant something which we can recognize, and which Aristotle would have recognized, as democracy; 'oligarchic' was with him a term of abuse; hence his insistence on the democratic element in the Roman system, although his experience of Rome, blending with his education in political philosophy, convinced him that a 'mixed' constitution was the best of all.

However, 'in practice the democratic principle was modified by a high minimum age (thirty years) for access to Assemblies; the absence of payment for attendance at Assemblies limited these to the richer classes; and office holding, as at Rome, was often expensive.' *

Polybios 28.7

(*At a meeting of the Council in 169*) Archon rose to speak in support of the envoys, for the matter called for the General's opinion; but after speaking briefly he left the Council Chamber; he wanted to avoid giving the impression of supporting a proposal from which he might derive personal profit, for his tenure of office had cost him a great deal of money.

Councillors, too, received no fees; at least, that seems to be the implication of another passage, from Polybios' account of a meeting of the Council in 187—a passage which is interesting also for what is said about the role of democracy.

---

* F. W. Walbank, *Historical Commentary on Polybius* I (1957), 222.

Polybios 22.11

The Council of the Achaians was holding one of its regular meetings, at Megalopolis. King Eumenes [4] had sent envoys to offer the Achaians a gift of 120 talents, on condition that they invested the money and used the interest to provide a fee for those attending regular meetings of the Federal Council ... When the envoys from Eumenes had been introduced, they reported his renewal of the alliance which his father had made with the Achaians, and announced to the meeting the King's offer of money. After they had spoken at length on these subjects, emphasizing the King's great goodwill and his generous feelings towards the Achaians, they brought their statement to a close.

After that, Apollonides of Sikyon rose to speak. So far as concerned the amount of money that was being offered, he said, the gift showed proper respect for the Achaians; but so far as the King's intention in offering the gift was concerned, and the purpose for which it was to be given, nothing could be more disgraceful and unconstitutional. For the laws forbade anyone, whether a private citizen or an official, to accept any gifts from a King on any pretext whatsoever. That they should all openly take a bribe by accepting the money would constitute a flagrant breach of the law; moreover, no one could deny that it would be most disgraceful. That the Council should be subsidized by Eumenes year after year, and should discuss public affairs after swallowing his bait, would be clearly shameful and harmful. Today Eumenes was offering money; next it would be Prusias, and then Seleukos.[5]

Kings and democracies were naturally opposed; most of their debates, and the most important, concerned their never-ending disputes with Kings ... He therefore called on the Achaians not merely to refuse the offer but to regard Eumenes with detestation for having thought of such a gift ... (*Another speaker then reminded the meeting of a long-standing grievance that the Achaians had against Eumenes.*) The great majority were so incensed that no one dared to speak in support of the King, and his offer was unanimously and vociferously rejected.

And another passage implies that the Councillors, by whom the Confederacy's officials, including the General, were elected, were for the most part men rich enough to own horses and serve in the cavalry.

Polybios 10.22

Most of those who are elected to the office of Commander of the Cavalry prove inadequate. Some, because of their own incapacity for conducting cavalry operations, dare not give the requisite orders even to their immediate subordinates. Others, whose hope is to attain the Generalship, canvass the young men with this in mind; their aim being to secure well-disposed supporters for the future, they do not find fault when they should.

Here, then, we have a democracy of which Aristotle would have approved, one in which poor citizens evidently did not exercise their right to participate to any great extent. But one can not be sure that Polybios consciously saw the merits of the Achaian system in quite that way. He seems to have been sincere in believing that the difference between a good democracy and a bad democracy, or between democracy and ochlocracy, depended on the moral qualities of its leaders. He had no understanding of social factors; social distress was something that would be of no consequence were it not exploited by evil men, 'disturbing the calm of the masses'.

ROMAN EXPANSION AND THE GREEK PEOPLES

It was in these moral terms that Polybios explained what, in his view, went wrong with Achaia's model democracy in the middle of the second century. At that time the Roman Senate had decided to weaken the Confederacy by detaching from it as many states as they could. A dispute between the Confederacy and the Spartans gave them an opening. Now, during the previous decades the gap between rich and poor in the Greek world had been widening, for various reasons, and there was growing distress among the poor. This had caused an increase of anti-Roman feeling, for the Romans, as suzerains, had generally lent their support to the most conservative of régimes (and, on occasion, to viciously self-seeking oppressors). So those leading Achaians who decided to resist Roman highhandedness evoked broader popular support than politicians of those days normally enjoyed.

Much of Polybios' history being lost, the first part of the story of what subsequently happened is known to us only from Pausanias, a patriotic Greek who in the second century A.D. wrote a guide for visitors to European Greece, including, like Baedeker, passages on the history of the various places. He tells us that when Roman envoys arrived at Corinth in 147, one of them, Lucius Aurelius Orestes, held a meeting at his lodgings.

Pausanias 7.14

He invited Diaios (*the General then in office*) and those who held office in each of the Achaian states to meet him. When they arrived, he disclosed to them the whole plan: that the Roman Senate had resolved that the Lakedaimonians should not be members of the Achaian Confederacy, nor should Corinth itself, and that Argos, Herakleia Oitaia, and the Arkadians of Orchomenos should also be detached from the Confederacy, for they were not kindred of the Achaians and all of them had joined the Confederacy later. While Orestes was explaining this, the Achaian officials rushed out of the house without waiting to hear the whole story and summoned the Achaians to Assembly. When the Achaians heard what the Romans had resolved, they turned against those Spartans who happened to be in Corinth at the time and arrested every one . . .

They also sent envoys to Rome to protest. Polybios tells us what happened subsequently. Another party of Roman envoys arrived to try to convince the Achaians of the error of their ways. Kritolaos, who had succeeded Diaios as General, at first played for time.

Polybios 38

9. He declared that he had no power to make any arrangements without the consent of the mass of the People. He would report to the Achaians at their next Assembly, which was due to be held in six months. Sextus and his fellow envoys realized that Kritolaos was being deliberately awkward; they were annoyed at his attitude . . . and returned to Italy, convinced that he was a fool and a madman.

After their departure, Kritolaos spent the winter travelling around the member states of the Confederacy and holding Assemblies in them, on the pretext that he wanted to give them an account of his discussions with the Lakedaimonians and with the Roman envoys; but in reality he wanted to indict the Romans and to put an unfavourable gloss on everything that they had said. As a result he worked up the masses into a mood of hostility and hatred. At the same time he instructed the officials to suspend the execution of public debts, not to take into custody people brought before them to be arrested for debt, and to let repayment of friendly-society loans be deferred until the war was over. Well, the effect of this demagogic performance was that everything that he said was believed, and the masses were ready to do whatever might be asked of them; for they could not foresee how things were bound to turn out, being caught by the bait of the gratifying relief that they were offered.

10. When Quintus Caecilius Metellus, who was in Macedon (*where he had been suppressing an anti-Roman movement*), heard about these developments and became aware of the confusion and disorder in the Peloponnese, he sent down his deputies, Gnaeus Papirius and Popilius Laenas the younger, and also Aulus Gabinius and Gaius Fannius. They happened to arrive in Corinth at the very moment at which the Achaians were meeting in Assembly; they were brought before the assembled People and delivered long conciliatory speeches, on the same lines as what had been said by Sextus and his fellow envoys: they made a great effort to dissuade the Achaians from adopting a more forthrightly hostile attitude towards the Romans, either on the grounds of their grievances against the Lakedaimonians or because of general feelings of illwill.

But the mass of the audience were not prepared to hear the envoys out: abuse was hurled at them and they were hooted and hustled out of the meeting. This was because a greater number of workers from factories and other sorts of menial employment had turned up than ever before; all the states of the Confederacy had caught this snivelling infection, in particular the entire population of Corinth. Only a few people fully approved of what the envoys said . . .[11]

So Kritolaos, who had inflamed the masses by his indictment of the Romans, persuaded the Achaians once more to vote for war, ostensibly against the Lakedaimonians but really against the Romans.

The great majority of the Achaians, rich and poor, now did all they could to support the war effort, but the Confederate army was of course very quickly overwhelmed.

Democracy and Empire: Alexander and After

Polybios 39.11

For my part I would be inclined to say that Fortune, wishing to preserve the Achaians somehow or other, had recourse to her last remaining trick, like a good wrestler: that is to say, bringing the Greeks to a quick and easy defeat. For that was why the indignation and fury of the Romans did not blaze out further.

Corinth was sacked and razed to the ground by the victorious Roman general, Mummius, male survivors killed, women and children sold into slavery; and when commissioners arrived from Rome to work with him:

He abolished democracies and substituted régimes based on property qualifications; tribute was levied, all Confederacies were dissolved, and a Roman governor was installed. Greece sank into more abject misery than ever before. (Pausanias 7.16–17)

Having been defeated, the member states of the Achaian Confederacy 'set up their rolls of honour, and we happen to possess that of Epidauros, 156 dead in the battle from one small town . . . Achaia had no cause to be ashamed of her last fight, and she was not ashamed'. *

* W. W. Tarn and G. T. Griffith, *Hellenistic Civilization* (1952), 35.

VI. The Perfect Democracy of the Roman Empire

A ROMAN VIEW OF GREEK DEMOCRACY

In 59, Cicero appeared for the defence at the trial in Rome of Lucius Valerius Flaccus, a member of a great noble family, who was charged with having practised extortion as governor of the Roman province of Asia—that is to say western Asia Minor, which was largely composed of Greek *poleis* that had once been sovereign republics. His speech shows that many Greek *poleis*, at least outside European Greece, were still democratic, formally and (if we allow for a barrister's rhetoric) perhaps quite effectively. It also gives us a Roman view of Greek democracy.

Cicero, *In Defence of Flaccus* 16–19

All Greek states are governed by impulsive votes taken while public meetings are in session. And to say nothing of present-day Greece, which has long since been dragged down into misery by the Greeks' own mismanagement, it was this one evil, the unrestrained and extravagant freedom of their public meetings, that brought about the destruction of the power, prosperity and glory that the Greeks at one time enjoyed.

When uneducated laymen who knew nothing whatsoever about affairs of state assembled in a theatre, they embarked on futile wars, they put troublemakers in charge of the government, they banished citizens who had done the state great service. If things of this kind were constantly happening at Athens in the days when people not only in Greece but in virtually all the world looked up to her, what restraints do you suppose are observed at public meetings nowadays in Phrygia or Mysia? Persons emanating from those regions often cause disturbances at public meetings here in Rome: what, then, do you expect to happen when they are on their own? ... How much effort does it cost to whip up factory workers and shopkeepers and all the dregs of the various communities, especially for an attack on a man who was recently in the highest authority over them but who for that very reason could not stand high in popular favour? If men loathe the apparatus of our rule, detest the very name of Rome and regard grazing-taxes and tithes and customs-duties as a curse, is it surprising that they are glad to seize any opportunity that may present itself to do us harm? So when you hear decrees read out, you must bear in mind that what you are hearing is not evidence. What you are hearing are the outbursts of an impulsive mob, the voices of men of no consequence, the babbling of ignorant laymen; the views of the most frivolous of nations, expressed at whipped-up public meetings.

MONARCHY AS TRUE DEMOCRACY

Already, however, by Cicero's time those who wrote in Greek often used the word *demokratia* to denote merely a constitutional régime, or a republic as distinct from a monarchy. And in the second century A.D., some writers who wished to flatter the Emperor went further. They claimed 'that the Empire represented the true, the perfect democracy ... because it gives each what is his due ... Even in the Republic liberty had actually involved the rule not of the People but for the People; now the power rested in different hands but care for the People's security was, if anything, increased ... It is perhaps not accidental that the further step of considering the Empire a perfect democracy because it assured economic and social justice may be found in the writings of men like Aelius Aristides, Philostratus and Dio Cassius—all Greek-speaking representatives of the broadly imperial rather than the narrowly Roman point of view.' *

Here, for instance, is the view that Philostratus (born *c.* A.D. 170), one of the circle of men of letters whom Julia Domna, the Syrian wife of the Emperor Septimius Severus, gathered round her, puts into the mouth of Apollonios of Tyana, a wandering Greek mystic, a pagan friar one might say, whose life, of which Philostratus wrote a highly imaginative account, spanned most of the first century A.D.

---

* Chester G. Starr, Jr, in *The American Historical Review* 58 (1952), 11ff. I have taken the title of his article as the title of this chapter.

Philostratus, *Life of Apollonios of Tyana* 5.35–36

'It seems to me, my friends, that you are wrong to try to unmake an Emperor when the issue is already decided; you are indulging in adolescent chatter at a time when swift action is demanded ... For my part, I don't care about this or that political system, for I follow the commandments of the gods; but I don't want to see the human flock perish for want of a just and prudent shepherd. For just as one man of outstanding ability can give democracy the appearance of government by a single person, the best of men, so government by a single person, if it provides for the welfare of the whole community, is democracy ...'

The Emperor (*Vespasian, who was on the point of assuming power in A.D. 69*) listened gladly to these remarks. 'Even if you had been living inside my mind, Apollonios,' he said, 'you could not have given a clearer account of my thoughts. So I shall be your disciple, for I believe that every word from your lips is divinely inspired. Teach me the duties of a good monarch'. . . .

In about A.D. 143, Aelius Aristides (*c.* A.D. 117–180), a wealthy littérateur from Smyrna, expressed similar sentiments in a eulogistic oration delivered to a select audience in Rome on the subject of the benefits which Roman rule had brought to the Mediterranean world. In this oration, the Roman Empire is referred to at times as if it were a Greek *polis* (and it was in a sense an enormously enlarged *polis*, with a citizen body spread over the whole of its vast territory), at times as if it were a confederacy of *poleis*, like Achaia in the days of Polybios (and so it was in a sense, although the *poleis* that it embraced were subject states, with no share in the central power).

In referring to the democratic element in the perfect mixed constitution that Rome has devised, Aristides is relying more than any other writer of the age who uses the word on the claim that the Empire gives the People, that is to say Roman citizens, what they want. And although his theorizing hardly deserves the respectful examination that it is sometimes given, one can allow that there is some justice in his claim, if one bears in mind that for the inhabitants of the Greek-speaking parts of the Empire (of whom Aristides is chiefly thinking throughout) this was its most prosperous age, and that in these parts Roman citizenship had been conferred mainly on individuals, rather than on whole communities as it had been in the western provinces, and mainly on men of wealth, like Aristides. That is the state of affairs to which his remarks on citizenship refer. In short, the Greek portion of the Empire was a democracy of 'the more gifted, the better bred and the more influential'.

Aristides, *To Rome*

90. It appears to me that in this Republic you have created a political system unlike any other known to mankind. In the past there were thought to be three political systems in the world: two of them had two names, each having reference to the character of those in control, despotism or kingship, oligarchy or aristocracy, while the third was called democracy, whether it was well or ill conducted. States had diverged, adopting one or another, as choice or chance decided in each case. Yours is quite unlike any other; it is, as it were, a blend of all political systems, without the faults associated with each; that is why it has come out on top. Thus when one considers the power of the People, observing how easily they get all they want and ask for, one will class it as a democracy, and will find nothing missing except the mistakes made by popular governments. And when one turns to the Senate, sitting in council and including the holders of office within its ranks, here, one will think, is an aristocracy in the strictest sense of the word. But when one's gaze turns to him who supervises and presides over the whole machinery of state, to whom the People owe their ability to get what they want, and from whom the few derive their influence and power, one sees a man who, in his exercise of absolute monarchy, exhibits none of the vices of a despot, a man raised above the august majesty of kingship . . .

59. Another thing which more than all the rest deserves consideration and admiration is your splendid policy with regard to citizenship. There has never been anything like it in the world. You have divided everyone in the Empire, which is to say the inhabited world, into two groups, and you have everywhere made the more gifted, the better bred and the more influential your fellow-citizens and even your kinsfolk, leaving the rest as subjects under your rule. Neither the sea nor distance overland bars the way to citizenship, nor is there any division between Europe and Asia: everything is open to everyone; no one is an alien who is worthy to hold office and be trusted. A democracy has been established embracing the world, under the rule and direction of

the best of men; all meet, as it were, in a common civic centre, where each will receive his deserts . . .

63. Being great, you have greatly extended your citizenship; you have not stood on your dignity and courted admiration by giving no one else a share. Instead you have looked for men worthy to man the ship of state, and you have made 'Roman' the name, not of a little republic, but of a widespread class: not one class among many, but one balancing all the rest. You have divided human kind not, as of old, into Greek and barbarian, but into Roman and non-Roman.

CITIES OF THE EMPIRE: THE ROLE OF THE PEOPLE

As we have seen, democracy, in a more normal sense of the term, had survived down into the first century B.C. as the vehicle of local government in a number of the Greek *poleis* that came under Roman control. If Augustus, the first emperor, had followed the advice which, according to Dio Cassius, his henchman Maecenas gave him in 29 B.C., it would have been completely abolished.

Dio Cassius 52.30

'In the communities that are under Roman control, the populace should have no authority in any matter, and should never convene in assembly, for no good would come of their deliberations, and they would constantly cause disturbances. It follows, in my opinion, that here in Rome likewise the populace should never assemble, either as a court of justice or for elections or in any other sort of meeting for the transaction of public business . . .'

But Dio, who, besides writing a *History of Rome*, was a loyal servant, in high office, of a series of emperors, from Commodus (A.D. 180-192) to Alexander Severus (A.D. 222-235), is here probably expressing his own views as to how things should be. Numerous surviving documents show that down to his time there continued to be at least some show of popular participation in some of the Greek *poleis* within the Empire. Decrees, for instance, still open with the formula 'Resolved by the Council and the People'. A document from Chalkis in Euboia, which is one of the latest to mention the People, is unusual in saying a little about the way in which the People participated. Its purpose is to record a dedication by a certain Aurelius Hermodorus.

W. Dittenberger, *Sylloge Inscriptionum Graecarum* (3rd edn, 1922), no. 898

With fortune's favour. In the term of office of Claudius Amiantos as Leader and of Lampros, son of the Temple Warden, as Chief Priest. Dedicated by Aurelius Hermodoros, appointed Temple Warden for life by decrees of the Council and Assembly on the motion of Amyntas, member of the Board of Ten, and Ulpius Pamphilus, in recognition of his construction of a wall around the temple and a precinct around the shrine, his enlargement of a portico and repair of the dilapidated portion, his building of a dining room and his provision of plants and trees, giving the Goddess fitting surroundings, to commemorate the award of the office of Temple Warden to himself and his children for life.

The decrees were passed in the term of office of Julius Mamertinus as Secretary and of Novius Lysanias, member for the first time of the Board of Ten, as General. The Councillors shouted: 'Thanks to Pamphilus for his motion. So be it.' Mamertinus, the Secretary, put a further motion: 'Whoever thinks that in conformity with your unanimous wish and the motion of his brother Pamphilus this honour should be given also to his children, let him raise his hand.' The Councillors shouted: 'Agreed!' So it was agreed.

Before the People Novius Lysanias, General for the second time, said: 'You do well to reward good men and to confer honours not only on them but also on their children, for only thus do we encourage others to render numerous services. This decree has already been passed by the Council. If you also agree, raise your hands.' The People shouted: 'Agreed!' So it was agreed. The People shouted: 'Long live the Temple Wardens!'

ACCLAMATION AND PROTEST

In this polite acclamation we have a foreshadowing of a new way in which the People's voice could make itself heard, in complaint as well as in praise—and sometimes effectively.

Codex Theodosianus 1.16.6

Emperor Constantinus Augustus to the Provincials:

... We grant to all the right on the one hand to praise by public acclamations governors who are most just and vigilant, to the end that we may bestow on them more rapid advancement, and on the other hand to indict those who are unjust and do harm, by raising their voices in complaint, to the end that the power of our censorship may remove them. For if these utterances are genuine and have not been spouted out to order by bodies of clients, we shall investigate them carefully: the Praetorian Prefects and *Comites* who have been stationed throughout the provinces shall bring to our knowledge the utterances of our provincials.

Given at Constantinople on the Kalends of November in the Consulship of Bassus and Ablabius (*November 1, A.D. 331*).

One place from which we have detailed evidence for the use of this right is Antioch in Syria, third city of the Empire, after Rome and Alexandria, with an urban population of some 200,000. We know more about life in Antioch in the fourth century than in any other city because we have the voluminous writings of Libanios: letters, speeches, and pamphlets in the guise of speeches.

Libanios (A.D. 314–c. 393) was a member of one of the wealthiest families in Antioch. From boyhood he was addicted to reading classical Greek literature and to writing Greek prose based on the best models; and, after teaching for a time at Constantinople and at Nicomedia, he spent the rest of his life, from the age of forty, at Antioch, purveying an old-fashioned classical education to the sons of rich citizens, though without neglecting his interests as a landowner. That he was on the imperial payroll as a professor gave him exemption from the burdens which others of his class had to assume as Councillors. At Antioch, as elsewhere, a self-perpetuating Council was what remained of local self-government, operating under the close control of the provincial governor and the *Comes Orientis*, overseer of the Levant as a whole.

Libanios, *Speech* 11 (*On Antioch*)

133. The whole structure of the city is founded upon the Council; it is the root upon which the city is based ... Its members can reckon up

The Perfect Democracy of the Roman Empire

fathers, grandfathers, great-grandfathers, and ancestors even more remote who have held the same rank. They have their forebears to teach them loyalty to the city, and as each man receives his inheritance, he understands that he must hold it for the community ... (*Libanios goes on to describe how generously they have spent on civic services their honestly gained and honourably inherited wealth, 'avoiding poverty by their prudence', and how their eloquence has successfully defended the city's freedom and gets from the imperial authorities whatever the Council wants.*) 150. Of the People, what greater thing could one say than that they are a fitting counterpart to the Council? ... (151) In the first place, each man of the People has a wife and children and all that goes to make up a home. These things have the power to teach prudence and devotion to a quiet life, whereas those who do not have any of them are apt to plunge into fierce disputes and violence..., as often happens in Egypt and in Italy, where some make every remark a pretext for a disturbance and others revel in the Council's difficulties. (152) But our People imitates the behaviour of children to their parents, and the Council imitates the role of a father to the People. It does not allow want to hit the commons. In return the commons pays to the Council the wages of nurture in goodwill, grieving at the Council's distress, rejoicing to the utmost at its good fortune ...

One notices the absence of that enthusiasm for the Empire as a whole that one finds in Aristides (whom, as a writer, Libanios deeply admired), although Libanios was in favour with the imperial authorities and although, or because, they now interfered much more. He 'sees the role of the Councillors as one of service to an ideal: the maintenance of Greek civilization'. The services they undertake 'make possible the survival at Antioch of the essential features of Greek city life . . .' But 'we may doubt whether the People's confidence in the Council was ever as great as he would have his readers believe'. * The People knew that decisive power lay in the hands of imperial officials, and they had a way of getting at them.

Libanios, *Speech* 29

2. When the People made such an extraordinary disturbance in the Theatre that they stopped the show and aroused fears that there was

* J. H. W. G. Liebeschuetz, *Antioch: City and Imperial Administration in the Later Roman Empire* (1972), 102, 208.

worse to come, their complaint being that the supply of bread to the city was not being properly attended to, the Governor, instead of using threats to put a stop to the disturbance, rose from his seat and said that he would do all that they wished.

(*But the shortage was so acute that on the following days the people fought over the available supplies.*) (4) These events emptied the city of Councillors: they fled to the countryside, not wanting to be burnt alive in their own houses; for that was what was expected.

On another occasion Libanios addresses the Emperor, Theodosius, complaining of what he sees as the foolish endeavours of a new Governor, Tissamenes, to get himself acclamations.

Libanios, *Speech* 33

11. When Tissamenes became Governor, Your Majesty, the People were aware of their limitations; he made them forget their limitations by leading them to believe that it was a great thing for the Governor to have words of praise shouted at him by them. The People were convinced that they governed their Governor and that by their insolence they had subordinated to themselves the man to whom they were by law subordinate: so they began trying to upset many established arrangements.

12. It is easy, Your Majesty, to prove that this is so. Something seems to have happened once in the Theatre to make the People silent. He regarded this as a disaster; his complexion, amongst other things, revealed this . . . Later, he was being escorted by some twenty individuals with whom one might have been ashamed to be seen; and as they were saying some of the usual things that better governors used to stop them saying, our fine friend descended from his carriage and said: 'Who gave you back your tongues? You didn't have them in the Theatre.' In saying this, he humiliated himself, revealing that he regarded their silence as damaging, their insults as an asset.

Libanios believed, or affected to believe, that all the acclamations, at least in the last years of his life, after 384, were organized by a group of about four hundred layabouts, superannuated prostitutes one and all, who were employed by the actors and dancers of the civic Theatre as a claque, but who also sold their services to officials with axes to grind. We do not need

The Perfect Democracy of the Roman Empire

to take this explanation too seriously (given Libanios' love of rhetorical exaggeration), but it must have contained a grain of truth; and the chanting of slogans does need to be well led to be effective. Libanios therefore urges Ikarios, *Comes Orientis* in A.D. 385, not to think that demonstrations in the Theatre are representative of the People of Antioch. (It should be noted, incidentally, that the People did not comprehend those, numbering perhaps four hundred thousand, mainly Syriac-speaking, who lived and worked in the surrounding countryside which was attached administratively to the city and in which the wealthy citizens had their estates.)

Libanios, *Speech* 26

5. So when some boorish incident occurs, don't regard it as the city's doing, my dear friend, regard it as the work of a very sick minority. When you lie awake at night, don't say to yourself 'That's what this city's like', say to yourself that that's what the worst element in the city is like . . .

(*Libanios goes on to belittle a fuss that was made because the Councillor responsible didn't get the water in the public baths hot enough, through shortage of funds.*) (8) So don't imagine that this disturbance was the city's doing. Those who have wives and children and homes and trades, and who live by their trades, are not the people who fill the Theatre; no, those who fill it are deserters from the army, slaves who don't see fit to slave, and, for the rest, a mob whose hopes of a livelihood are pinned to the stage. If there are any decent people in the audience, they are pushed in the same direction by this element: when they have wanted to praise the Governor, they have been prevented, and when they have wanted to escape they have been forced to stay. The instructions that compel them to say what they should not and not say what they should emanate from that small group of which I have spoken. So one can accurately say that the opposition to you amounts to very little.

But as Libanios admits, sadly or indignantly, the slogans were often heeded. True democracy?

Notes

CHAPTER I

1. Son of the famous Perikles.
2. The Controller of this Fund seems to have been an elected official, and was perhaps able to exercise supervision over revenue and expenditure in general.
3. The word *demos* is used here, as often, to mean the whole citizen body. Sometimes, on the other hand, it is used to mean the common people as distinct from an élite of whatever kind.
4. Here and in subsequent invocations of the law—*ho nomos*—during this episode, it is not clear what particular law, if any, is in question. Probably the procedure objected to was merely unprecedented, and was felt by some to be illegal in the sense of being contrary to the established practice of the democratic régime, but by others to be within the People's power to prescribe. This illustrates the uncertainty at this time about the nature and status of *nomos*: see pp. 18ff.
5. A board of officials, chosen annually by lot, who were, *inter alia*, in charge of the prison and of executions.
6. In 403, supporters of democracy seized control of the Peiraieus, the port of Athens, during the rule of the junta of the Thirty, who had come to power in Athens with Spartan backing in 404.
7. This requirement was imposed, on the motion of Perikles, in 451–450; previously, to have a citizen father had sufficed.
8. The demes (*demoi*: yet another use of the word *demos*) were the basic local civic units (cf. parishes, townships, wards); membership was hereditary. They were grouped into ten constituencies (*phylai*: often misleadingly translated 'tribes') in a complicated way, to ensure that each constituency included demes situated in different parts of Attica: see chapter III.
9. Aristotle often speaks of 'the Court of Justice' when he means one of the several Courts (see pp. 11, 28ff.).
10. If the finding is that he is not of free birth: not, presumably, if it is found merely that he is not of citizen parentage.

11. It had become accepted at Athens that at least one elected official was needed to supervise revenues and expenditure. When Aristotle wrote, the two Treasurers he names shared this rôle.

12. The Presiding Committee were called *prytaneis*; the period for which a committee officiated was called *prytaneia*, commonly rendered 'prytany'. The Tholos was a circular building on one side of the civic centre, the Agora, adjacent to the Council House, the Bouleuterion. Agora—an open square often surrounded by public buildings, like the Roman Forum—and Bouleuterion were features of every Greek *polis*.

13. Evidence shows that by this time the great majority of citizens could read and write: see F. D. Harvey, 'Literacy in the Athenian Democracy', *Revue des études grecques* 79 (1966), 585–635.

14. Laying an impeachment—*eisangelia*—was a procedure for initiating swift action against a person alleged to be guilty of a grave crime against the community.

15. Under a law enacted after a period of dictatorship in the sixth century, 'because of distrust of outstandingly influential persons, seeing that Peisistratos had established himself as a dictator when he was a popular leader and a general' (Aristotle): the citizen against whom the largest number of his fellow citizens voted (each writing a name on an *ostrakon*, a scrap of broken pottery), provided that there were at least six thousand votes in all (or, on another view, against him), had to go into exile for ten years. After 443 an ostracism is known to have been held only once, in about 417; prosecution was the expedient that came to be used in its stead.

16. In the fifth century all the Stewards' functions had been discharged by the Presiding Committee. Presumably it came to be felt that this gave them too much power, even if only for one tenth of the year.

17. When the citizen body was grouped into ten constituencies, c. 508 (see chapter III), the Delphic oracle was invited to select the ten Attic heroes (legendary mortals revered as superhuman) after whom they should be named, e.g. Erechtheis after Erechtheus. Statues of these 'eponymous' heroes stood in the Agora.

18. Thirty, later forty, deme judges, chosen annually by lot (and so called because formerly they had toured round the demes), were responsible for dealing with private suits of various kinds; three or four of them dealt with those in which the defendant was of their constituency.

19. Use of the lot had begun in 486; previously these offices, particularly that of Archon, had been the ones for which young men who aspired to political prominence had competed.

20. These questions, handed down from early times when only landowners were citizens, were to ascertain whether a man was really a citizen. By Aristotle's time a citizen might not have such household altars of his own; but he would normally belong to a religious association, a phratry,

that maintained them on behalf of all its members. A citizen's mother would not have been on the roll of a deme, as only males were entered on the rolls.

21. From 457, the Archonships were legally open to members of all but the lowest (fourth) property class, the *thetes*; and the same probably applied to all offices. 'But nowadays when someone who is going to be included in the drawing of lots for some office is asked to what class he belongs, no one would say "the *thetes*".' (Aristotle, *Constitution of Athens* 7)

22. There were six obols to a drachma, a hundred drachmas to a mina, six thousand drachmas to a talent. A man could expect to receive about a drachma for a day's work, skilled or unskilled. Given the great differences between ancient and modern modes of life, it is impossible to state what this represents in present-day money.

23. The best-known example is that of Perikles, elected General annually from 443 to 429 (but his powers were no greater than those of any of the other nine Generals).

24. The various officials 'brought into court' all cases within their sphere of competence that they had decided at a preliminary inquiry to be admissible, and presided over the hearing.

25. Probably to help in raising the alarm, perhaps also to clear space for mobilization of forces.

26. The low hill, west of the Akropolis and south-west of the Agora, on which the People normally met in Assembly.

27. It was in that event that an Examination on the lines indicated was held.

28. In addition to the two walls built, *c.* 461–456, linking Athens and its harbours, Peiraieus and Phaleron (see chapter III), a second parallel wall to the Peiraieus was built *c.* 445, constituting 'the middle wall'.

29. Brother of Plato's mother; later one of the leaders of the junta of Thirty; killed in the democratic counter-revolution in 403.

30. Women, and shoemakers, did not spend as much time in the sun as most men.

31. The Stoa Basileios or Royal Portico, one of the porticoes flanking the Agora; so called because the Basileus officiated there. Part of the code, engraved on stone slabs attached to the rear walls, has been found.

32. At Athens the year was divided into twelve months (Hekatombaion being the first) as well as being divided, from 508, into ten prytanies for administrative purposes.

33. 382–381 (the Athenian year began at midsummer). This was the customary way of indicating the date of events.

34. Pasion (died 370) was originally a slave. After working as a clerk in a bank, he was freed by the owner and became Athens' leading banker

Notes

(a career neither typical for a slave nor wholly exceptional). He handed on his bank, and, by his will, his widow, to his own freed slave Phormion.

35. In the case of the many crimes for which the penalty was not fixed by law, jurors who found a defendant guilty had to go on to choose between the penalties proposed by the prosecutor and the defendant.

36. His civic rights would have been suspended until he paid.

37. Untrue: it was only marriage to aliens that was forbidden.

38. It was normal for a child born of wedded Athenian parents to be enrolled in his father's phratry, a 'brotherhood' united by worship of a supposed common ancestor.

39. In what circumstances we do not know. Perhaps boys whom the Council, after examination, declared not to have reached the age of eighteen could appeal to a Court.

40. A maximum figure, assuming that all six thousand were in session on all the three hundred or so days which were neither holidays nor days of meetings of the Assembly.

41. A parody of an oath of loyalty to democracy such as had to be taken in various contexts.

42. Silphion, a medicinal herb, was one of the chief crops and exports of the Greek state Kyrene in Libya, which was unusual in still having a royal house, whose founder and many of his successors were named Battos.

43. The original function of a tripod was to support a cauldron over a fire; but tripods, usually of bronze, became a common form of thank-offering to gods.

44. Captains of warships, trierarchs, were provided by the state with the hull and the necessary equipment—which they had to return in good condition at the end of the season unless it had been damaged by enemy action—and with the crew's pay and rations; but they had to spend a certain amount, and might spend a great deal, on improving the equipment, hiring skilled professional officers, effecting running repairs, and (especially in the fourth century, when the state was poor) making up pay and rations. After 411 the burden was often shared between two citizens, the level of qualifying wealth being probably lowered; and from 357 there was a scheme to spread the burden over all men of means every year; but, in 340, Demosthenes (himself a very rich man, his father having owned manufactories of knives and beds) got it shifted on to the shoulders of the really rich.

45. On these two concepts of equality, see below, chapter IV, p. 99.

CHAPTER II

1. Lakedaimon was a designation that comprehended both Sparta and the communities of the *Perioikoi*, but since the *Perioikoi* had to comply with decisions made by the Spartiates about alliances and wars, there is some justification for referring to the Assembly of Spartiates as 'the Lakedaimonian Assembly' in this context. There was in fact no circumstance in which Spartiates and *Perioikoi* assembled together.

2. The official line at Sparta from the fifth century onwards was that all the existing political and social institutions and rules had been established in the remote past by a legislator named Lykurgos. Aristotle is sceptical, and usually refers non-committally to 'the legislator'.

3. Spartiates generally tried to have small families, with only one son, as the family land had to be divided equally between sons. So if a son was killed in war or died young, there might be only a daughter as heir.

4. Already by 371 Spartiate numbers had so declined that they could field only about 1,500 'Equals', whereas they sent 5,000 in 479 against the Persians.

5. The Council of Elders, *Gerousia*, consisted of twenty-eight Elders, aged over 60, holding office until they died, together with the two Kings. Vacancies were filled by election, but Aristotle tells us that members were all drawn from a small ring of families, who thus, with the two royal families, dominated Spartan life. Such men could be called 'those best qualified', for only they had any experience of running things; rank and file Equals had generally learnt only to obey.

6. Voting at the election of Ephors was presumably again a matter of seeing who could shout loudest, as we are told it was at the election of Elders.

7. Every Spartiate had to take his main meal of the day at a communal mess, to ensure constant readiness for military service.

8. Aristotle is presumably referring to their position after defeating the Athenians in 405; they had been regarded as in some sense leaders or champions of the Greeks as early as 550.

CHAPTER III

1. From the later years of the fifth century this became a slogan, some using it to refer to full democracy, which they wished to maintain, others, who did not like full democracy, but did not consider themselves or did not wish to be thought anti-democratic, using it to refer to what they believed the system to have been in the time of Solon or Kleisthenes (see, for instance, Isokrates' remarks in chapter IV, pp. 98ff.).

Notes

2. Solon gave citizens who were tried and sentenced by officials, which was how most offences were then dealt with, the right to appeal to 'the Heliaia', which probably then meant, however, not a Court with a large panel of jurors, as it did later, but the Assembly. Subsequent growth of the habit of appealing evidently led first to the creation of popular Courts of Appeal and then to these becoming courts of first instance.

3. By a measure of 462, perhaps followed by others, depriving it of all except certain religious functions.

4. Even the poorest of citizens could and often did serve in the navy, but only those who had the means to equip themselves with the arms and armour of a hoplite, a heavy-armed infantryman, were called on for land fighting.

5. Aristotle seems to think that the right to hear appeals (see note 2) did not constitute 'power'.

6. At the time at which this pamphlet was written, there were probably about 30,000 aliens resident at Athens, compared with about 170,000 Athenians, men, women and children. The size of the slave population is much harder to estimate, but it was probably not less than 100,000. In most other democratic states the proportion of aliens and of slaves was probably somewhat smaller.

7. The author does not mean that decent Athenians ought to emigrate; he is referring to immigrants.

CHAPTER IV

1. The ships gave Darius an excuse, or a reason, for sending an expedition to Greece in 470 to punish the Athenians; Xerxes subsequently made a greater effort to avenge this defeat; and the fact that both Sparta and Athens played a leading part in resisting Xerxes led to rivalry and conflict between them.

2. *Isonomia* was probably the word used to denote democracy down into the fifth century, before the word *demokratia* came into use. The word translated in this passage as 'the People' is not *demos* but *plethos*. At this time *plethos* seems to have covered all who belonged to the community, whereas *demos* denoted rather 'the commons'; but by Aristotle's time *plethos* had acquired a different sense—'the masses', as distinct from men of quality.

3. Or 'without reference to his turn in the queue'. It is not certain which of these two ideas Thucydides meant to convey.

4. In Athens the stock-in-trade of those who made a living as fortune tellers was not 'what the stars foretell' nor what could be read in a customer's palm but what were alleged to be oracles.

5. 'A man of quality' has something of the requisite ambivalence as a translation of *kalos kagathos*, which is a term commonly used of a member of the gentry as such but means also that the man so described (it is never used of a woman) is admirable, and capable of doing what people expect of him.

6. The Thirty, who ruled Athens 404–403.

7. The financial reserve with which the Athenians had entered the war was now almost completely exhausted, and revenues had been greatly reduced, for recently the Peloponnesians had detached many of the tributary allies and had installed a permanent force in Attica, which put a stop to the mining of silver.

8. *Kaloi kagathoi* again. Many of those in the oligarchic movement thought themselves such: Phrynichos was a man of modest origin.

CHAPTER V

1. 'Thousands' were the constituencies into which the citizens of Samos were divided for administrative purposes.

2. 'Stater' was the word denoting the standard coin of a state. In Samos it had been since the fifth century a two-drachma silver piece: enough to keep a family for a day or two.

3. 'Lakonians' was an unofficial abbreviation of Lakedaimonians, the term embracing Spartiates and *Perioikoi*.

4. King of Pergamon, a wealthy state in western Asia Minor. Some eighty years previously, the ruler of Pergamon had thrown off the suzerainty of the Seleukids—the kings, descended from one of Alexander's generals, who ruled much of his empire in Asia.

5. Prusias was the ambitious king of Bithynia, a land in north-western Asia Minor. Seleukos was Seleukos IV.

Index

Names

Achaia, Achaians 109ff., 120
Aischines 12, 27
Aischylos 16, 78, 82
Alexander 103, 107, 135
Alkibiades 70, 93f., 102f.
Andokides 20
Antioch 107, 124ff.
Apollonios of Tyana 119f.
Areopagus, Council of the 57, 61, 97ff.
Aristides, Aelius 119ff., 125
Aristophanes 15, 18, 29, 31, 56, 82, 87ff.
Aristotle xxi, 6ff., 23, 27, 29, 32, 36, 38, 46f., 49, 51, 53, 56ff., 61ff., 71f., 84, 99, 103ff., 107, 112, 114, 129ff., 133f.
Athens, Athenians xxf., I *passim*, 50, IV–V *passim*, 107, 118, 133
Cicero 23, 99, 118f.
Delphi 18, 49f., 75, 130
Demokritos 85
Demosthenes 11f., 20ff., 27f., 132
Dio Cassius 119, 122
Ephialtes 61
Euripides 82, 105
Four Hundred, The 18f., 96f., 102f., 135
Gorgias 13f., 97
Herodotos 79ff.
Hesiod 43ff.
Homer 39ff., 94
Isokrates 73, 97ff., 133
Kleisthenes 55, 62f., 78, 98f., 133
Kleon 29, 31, 55f., 70, 82, 89, 92, 101
Lakedaimonians *see* Spartans
Libanios 124ff.

Pausanias 115, 117
Peiraieus 6, 33, 64, 89, 96, 129, 131
Peisistratos 55f., 59, 62
Peloponnesian War 65, 71f., 82, 85, 97, 100f.
Perikles 13, 19, 33, 55f., 61, 70f., 73, 82f., 85ff., 92ff., 105, 129, 131
Philip 11, 103, 107
Philostratus, Flavius 119f.
Phrynichos 96, 102f., 135
Pindar 77f.
Plato 13f., 56, 65, 76, 84, 87, 99, 103ff., 109, 131
Plutarch 76
Pnyx 12, 16, 90ff., 131
Polybios 109ff., 120
Protagoras 83ff.
Rhodes 38
Rome, Romans xixf., 112, 114ff., VI *passim*
Samos 102, 108, 135
Socrates 4, 13ff., 65, 84, 92ff., 105
Solon 32, 55ff., 98, 134
Sparta, Spartans xx, 1, 5, 18, 47ff., 62, 64f., 68, 70ff., 80, 100, 102f. 110, 115, 129, 133ff.
Syracuse 76, 77, 87f.
Themistokles 13, 55f., 63f.
Thirty, The 18f., 33, 71, 93, 95ff., 129, 131, 135
Thucydides 29, 56, 63f., 70f., 82, 85ff., 100ff.
Tyrtaios 47ff.
Xenophon 1f., 14, 19, 65, 73ff., 92, 100

Subjects

Acclamation 123f., 125ff.

Index

Agora 11, 53, 90, 105, 130f.
Aliens xvii, 7, 23ff., 33, 45, 63, 67f., 73f., 86, 107, 121, 132, 134
Aristocracy 44, 52, 61, 73, 81f., 87, 99, 109, 121; *see also* Nobles
Assembly 1ff., 7f., 10ff., 20ff., 24ff., 37, 40ff., 50, 54, 66f., 69, 72, 76, 77ff., 87ff., 93f., 100f., 104ff., 108, 111f., 115f., 118f., 122f., 130ff.
Autonomy xvii, 100f., 103, 107, 109, 111, 114f.
Boule see Council
Bribery 9f., 33, 69, 72, 82, 106, 113
Citizens, citizenship 14f., 17f., 21f., 29, 32f., 36, 41, 46f., 48ff., 52, 59, 61ff., 65ff., 71ff., 74f., 79f., 82ff., 88, 91ff., 96ff., 104ff., 107f., 111f., 116f., 118f., 122ff.
Citizenship, grants of 23ff., 63, 107, 121f.; qualifications for 6, 23ff., 37, 52, 63, 84f., 129ff.
Civic rights, loss of 11, 24f., 63, 96
Commons xviif., xx, 31, 38, 39, 53f., 56ff., 65ff., 71f., 73, 76, 77f., 81f., 88f., 94, 100f., 104ff., 109, 115f., 119, 125
Confederacy 110ff., 120
Constituencies 3, 7, 9, 11, 62f., 129f., 135
Council 2f., 5, 6ff., 11f., 20f., 24, 28, 30, 50, 61f., 67, 69, 72, 75, 88, 90, 96f., 99, 110ff., 123, 124f., 127, 130, 132, 133; *see also* Elders, Senate
Craftsmen xvi, 12, 13f., 15, 16f., 54, 63, 68, 84f., 89, 91, 92, 105, 116, 127
Debt xxf., 57ff., 116
Decrees 4f., 17ff., 24, 27f., 72, 76, 79, 100f., 108, 118f., 123; *see also* Law, Legislation
Defence xviif., 7, 11f., 13, 16, 24f., 28, 33ff., 40, 43f., 46ff., 51ff., 61, 63ff., 65f., 68ff., 71, 74f., 76, 80, 88, 100ff., 107, 111, 114ff., 132ff.
Demes 6, 9f., 20, 25, 62f., 129f.
Demokratia xv, 38, 78, 112, 119, 134
Demos 46f., 89, 129, 134
Dictatorship xviii, 51, 56, 58f., 62, 70, 74, 76, 77f., 80ff., 88, 93f., 98, 107, 121, 130

Education 13f., 53, 67, 81, 83, 87, 90, 93, 98, 105, 118, 125, 130
Ekklesia see Assembly
Elders 40, 50ff.
Election 2, 6, 9, 20, 22, 27f., 52, 57, 61f., 66, 98f., 104, 112ff.
Embezzlement 2, 9, 30, 33, 71, 91f.
Emperors, Roman 119ff., 122, 124, 126
Empire, Athenian 31, 64, 69f., 72, 100ff.
Roman 117, 118ff., 125
Equality xxii, 36ff., 53, 59, 63, 76, 80, 83, 86, 88, 98f., 104, 106, 110f., 132, 133
Eunomia 49ff., 61, 63, 67
Family *see* Household
Farmers *see* Peasants
Fees 7, 10, 16, 21, 29, 31, 36, 37f., 61, 65, 68, 71f., 75, 99, 112f.
Financial administration 2, 6, 8f., 24, 27, 31, 35, 55, 69f., 73ff., 88, 108
Fines 2, 8f., 23, 24f., 32, 35, 92, 96, 108f.
Freed slaves xix, 53f., 68, 107, 132
Freedom *see* Liberty
Generals 2ff., 6, 10, 11, 12, 27, 37, 41ff., 66, 70, 88, 90, 102, 111ff., 115f.
Governors, Roman 116f., 118f., 124, 126f.
Grain supply 1, 7, 16f., 108f., 125f.
Helots xx, 47, 49, 51, 53f., 68, 74
Hoplites xvii, 46f., 64f., 134; *see also* Defence, Military Service
Horseowners 46f., 65, 74f., 76, 89, 91f., 114
Household xvii, 3, 7, 10, 12, 39ff., 86f., 125, 127, 130f., 133; *see also* Inheritance, Women
Inheritance 7, 12, 28, 52ff., 133
Isonomia 38, 63, 81, 134
Jurors *see* Law Courts
Justice 2, 44ff., 59, 68, 83, 86, 99, 104, 106, 120, 124; *see also* Law Courts
Kaloi kagathoi 135
Kings, kingship xviff., 39ff., 46, 49f., 51f., 53, 74, 79, 80, 81ff., 102f., 107, 111, 113, 120f.; *see also* Emperors

Index

Knights *see* Horseowners
Labourers 83, 105, 116, 119
Land, landowners 47, 49, 51ff., 55f., 57ff., 64, 76, 77, 88f., 124, 127; *see also* Peasants
Law xix, 2, 4f., 6ff., 10, 12f., 18ff., 33f., 49, 51, 57f., 60f., 83, 86, 88, 92ff., 98, 110, 113, 126; *see also* Decrees, Legislation
Law Courts 2, 5, 6, 8ff., 12f., 18, 19, 21ff., 61, 71f., 89, 92, 95, 99, 108, 110, 122; *see also* Prosecution
Leaders, leadership xviiiff., 2ff., 12ff., 31, 40ff., 53f., 55f., 57f., 61f., 63f., 70f., 73, 77f., 82f., 87f., 89ff., 93, 96, 100ff., 104f., 111ff., 115f., 120f., 126f.
Legislation 8, 19ff., 51f., 58f., 60f., 62f., 69, 83, 88, 93f., 98, 133; *see also* Decrees
Libertas xix
Liberty xxii, 36f., 67, 71, 76, 80, 82f., 86, 98, 103, 105, 110f., 118, 119; *see also* Autonomy
Liturgies *see* Services, Public
Lot 2, 6ff., 11, 24, 27f., 29, 37, 63, 66, 81, 92, 98f., 130
Manufacturers 33, 55, 132; *see also* Craftsmen
Masses *see* Commons
Merchants *see* Trade
Military service 10, 12, 30, 31, 39, 41ff., 45ff., 52f., 64ff., 71, 74f., 80, 116f., 134
Monarchy *see* Dictatorship, Kingship
Navy, 1ff., 28, 31, 33ff., 55, 63ff., 68f., 71, 75, 76, 80, 100, 102, 132
Nobles, Notables xviff., xixf., 2, 29, 39ff., 55f., 57, 60ff., 65f., 70, 76, 77, 80, 85, 89, 92, 102, 104, 121, 133
Nomos xviii, 45f., 51, 62, 129; *see also* Law
Oaths 5, 6, 10, 21, 24, 31
Office, qualifications for 11, 37, 52, 57, 62, 66, 86, 88, 99, 106, 112, 131; *see also* Tests
Officeholders, accountability of 2f., 7ff., 27f., 30, 37, 61, 69, 81, 96, 98f.; role of 2, 8f., 11, 27f., 29, 31, 37, 52ff., 108f., 111f., 123, 129f., 131; *see also* Generals; Services, Public
Oligarchy 22, 44, 46, 52, 57, 61, 69, 80, 81f., 88, 93f., 96f., 99, 101, 102f., 104, 107, 112, 117; *see also* Four Hundred, Thirty
Oratory 2, 13f., 15f., 40ff., 70, 77f., 83, 93, 97, 116
Ostracism 7, 130
Paternalism, patronage 41, 43f., 50, 59, 62, 77, 82, 87, 98, 120f., 125
Peasants xviif., 15, 17, 32, 39, 44, 49, 54, 57ff., 62, 88f., 104
People *passim*; *see also* Demos, Plethos
Phratries 25, 130f., 132
Phylai 8; *see also* Constituencies
Plethos 134
Polis xv, xviiff., and *passim*
Politicians 2, 15, 29, 38, 94; *see also* Leaders, Oratory
Poor, poverty xx, 25, 30, 35, 37, 38, 47, 49, 51f., 57f., 64, 66, 68, 73, 76, 82f., 85, 86, 94, 106, 114
Population 47, 52, 87, 110, 124, 127, 133, 134
Property, confiscation of 3ff., 7, 25, 31, 32, 35, 96
Prosecution, prosecutors 2ff., 6ff., 13, 19ff., 23ff., 27, 28ff., 31ff., 54, 61, 70, 92, 95ff., 98f., 103, 104
Punishment, capital 3ff., 8, 23, 101, 103
Representation 111f.
Revolutions, revolutionary Movements xviii, 18, 59, 62f., 76, 92f., 96, 102, 106, 125f.
Salaries *see* Fees
Senate 121
Serfs xvii, xx, 51, 57f., 60f.; *see also* Helots
Services, Public 33ff., 68f., 97, 108, 123, 125, 127, 132
Silvermining xxi, 31, 55, 63, 74, 135
Slaves xvii, xxff., 6, 31, 37, 58, 60f., 63, 67f., 74, 76, 89, 101, 107, 127, 132, 134; *see also* Helots, Serfs
Soldiers, professional xvi, xviii, 62, 76, 107, 127, 132

Strategoi see Generals
Sykophantai 32f.; *see also* Prosecutors
Taxation 31, 33f., 69f., 74, 85, 97, 117, 119
Tests 6, 8ff., 12f., 24, 26, 28ff., 34, 69, 96, 130f.
Trade, Traders xvi, xviii, 12, 15, 16f., 23, 32, 74, 89, 105, 119, 127
Voting 2, 3ff., 6ff., 10f., 17f., 19, 20, 21f., 24, 26, 27, 76, 79f., 91f., 100, 106, 109, 112, 113, 116, 118f., 123

War *see* Generals, Military service, Navy, Peloponnesian War
Wealth, private xx, 1, 6f., 28, 30, 32ff., 51f., 57ff., 62, 66, 68, 70, 74f., 76, 82f., 85, 86, 88, 94, 95, 97ff., 104, 108, 112f., 114, 120f., 124ff., 132
Women xvii, 7, 10, 12, 15ff., 24ff., 30, 40f., 42, 52, 57, 78f., 101, 117, 125, 127, 131, 135